THE
FOURTH
DIMENSION

David(Paul) Yonggi Cho

Seoul Logos Co., Inc.

DEDICATION

This book is dedicated to the many
     ...seeking
          ...searching,
               ...and struggling
to find and walk a consistent road of faith in their
Christian lives.

The Fourth Dimension

Printed in Seoul Korea by Seoul Logos Co., Inc.
Yoido Full Gospel Church
Yoido P. O. Box 7
Seoul, Korea

TABLE OF CONTENTS

gratis

115660

FOREWORD

I count it a great honor to write these words as a foreword to this exciting book by my brother in Christ, David (Paul) Yonggi Cho. I am personally indebted to him for spiritual strength, and for insights I have received from God through this great Christian pastor.

I was ministering to his huge congregation in Seoul, Korea, when we received a telephone call that our daughter was tragically injured in a horrible traffic accident in Iowa. Accompanying us to the plane as my wife and I left in haste was our dear friend, David Yonggi Cho, prayerfully supporting and sustaining us. And when I arrived some hours later to sit through the black night hours at the pain-wracked side of my daughter, whose left leg had just been amputated and whose life had just been snatched from death, I found myself reading page after page of the unpublished manuscript of this book for which I now, with enthusiasm, offer a word or two.

I discovered the reality of that dynamic dimension in prayer that comes through visualizing the healing experience. Line after line of the original manuscript was underlined by this travel-weary pastor, this suffering father. I can only hope and pray that many Christians—and unbelievers too—will find this book coming into their hands and drawing from it the amazing spiritual truths that its pages contain.

Don't try to understand it. Just start to enjoy it! It's true. It works. I tried it. Thank you—David Yonggi Cho—

for allowing the Holy Spirit to give this message to us and to the world. God loves you and so do I!

Robert H. Schuller

PREFACE

This book was written in 1979, approximately fifteen years ago from today. At that time I had 50,000 members but now God has given us 700,000 members.

When I perused my old book, amazingly I have nothing to change very drastically in its contents.

Of course, in many places I found immature thoughts and erroneous expressions that could cause misunderstanding. Since English is my second language, I sometimes have a great difficulty to express the exact nuance of my beliefs—and it was worse in 1979.

So, I decided to rewrite some portions of my book to make the thoughts clearer than before. I also want to add more about the law of faith and spiritual truths that I have found during these fifteen years.

My sincere desire is to see as many people as possible helped and encouraged in their spiritual odyssey in this great walk of faith with our Lord Jesus Christ!

David(Paul) Yonggi Cho, Pastor
Yoido Full Gospel Church
Seoul, Korea
November, 1996

INTRODUCTION

Life Full and Free

In the chaos that followed the Korean Conflict, I was among the many struggling for existence. Poor but persistent, I held several jobs in the course of a single day.

One afternoon I was working as a tutor. Suddenly I felt something oozing up from deep inside my chest. My mouth felt full and I thought I would choke.

As I opened my mouth, blood began to gush out. I tried to stop the bleeding, but blood continued to flow from my nostrils and mouth. My stomach and chest soon filled with blood. Severely weakened, I fainted.

When I returned to consciousness everything seemed to be spinning. Shaken, I barely managed to travel back home.

I was nineteen years old and I was dying.

Go Home, Young Man

Frightened, my parents immediately sold enough of their possessions to take me to a famous hospital for treatment. The doctor's examinations were careful. Their diagnosis: incurable tuberculosis.

When I heard their assessment, I realized how badly I wanted to live. My desires for the future were to end before I even had the chance to start fully living.

Desperate, I turned to the physician who had pronounced the grim diagnosis. "Doctor," I pleaded. "Isn't there anything you can do for me?"

His reply was to resound often in my mind. "No. This type of tuberculosis is very unusual. It is spreading so fast that there is no way to arrest it."

"You have three, at the most four months to live. Go home, young man. Eat anything you want. Say good-bye to your friends."

Dejected, I left the hospital. I passed hundreds of refugees on the streets, and felt a kindred spirit. Feeling totally alone, I was one of the hopeless.

I returned home in a dazed condition. Ready to die, I hung a three month calendar on the wall. I was raised a Buddhist. I prayed daily that Buddha would help me but no hope came and I grew continually worse.

Sensing that my time to live was shortening, I gave up faith in Buddha. It was then that I began to cry to the unknown God. Little did I know how great an impact His response would have on my life.

Touching Tears

A few days later, a high-school girl visited me and

began to talk about Jesus Christ. She told me about Christ's virgin birth, His death on a cross, His resurrection and salvation through grace. These stories seemed nonsense to me. I neither accepted her stories nor paid much attention to this ignorant young female. Her departure left me with one emotion: relief.

But the next day she returned. She came again and again, every time troubling me with stories about the God-man, Jesus. After more than a week of these visits, I became greatly agitated, and roughly rebuked her.

She did not run away in shame, nor retaliate in anger. She simply knelt down and began to pray for me. Large tears rolled down her cheeks, reflecting a compassion foreign to my well-organized and sterile Buddhist philosophies and rituals.

When I saw her tears, my heart was deeply touched. There was something different in this young girl. She was not reciting religious stories to me; she was living what she believed. Through her love and tears I could feel the presence of God.

"Young lady," I entreated, "please don't cry. I am sorry. I now know about your Christian love. Since I am dying, I will become a Christian for you."

Her response was immediate. Her face brightened into a glow and she praised God. Shaking hands with me, she gave me her Bible.

"Search the Bible," she instructed. "If you read it faithfully you will find the words of life."

That was the first time in my life I had ever held a Bible. Constantly struggling to gasp air into my lungs, I opened to the book of Genesis.

Turning the pages to Matthew, she smiled: "Sir, you are so sick that if you start from Genesis, I don't think you will last long enough to finish Revelation. If you start from the book of Matthew, you will have enough time."

Expecting to find deep moral and philosophical religious teachings, I was shocked at what I was reading. "Abraham begat Isaac; Isaac begat Jacob; and Jacob begat Judas and his brethren."

I felt foolish. I closed the Bible saying, "Young lady, I won't read this Bible. This is only a story of one man begetting another. I would rather read a telephone directory."

"Sir," she replied. "You don't recognize these names right now. But as you read on, these names will come to hold a special meaning for you." Encouraged, I began reading the Bible again.

The Living Lord

As I read I did not find any systematized philosophies, any theories of medical science or any religious rituals. But I did find one striking theme: The Bible constantly talked about Jesus Christ, the Son of God.

The imminence of my death had brought me to the realization that I needed something greater than a religion, greater than a philosophy, and even greater than sympathy for the trials of human existence. I needed someone who could share my struggles and sufferings, someone who could give me victory.

Through reading the Bible, I discovered that Someone to be the Lord Jesus Christ.

The Person Jesus Christ was not bringing a religion, a code of ethics, nor a series of rituals. In a profoundly practical way, Jesus was bringing salvation to humanity. Hating sin, Christ loved the sinner, accepting all who came to Him. Deeply aware of my sins, I knew I needed His forgiveness.

Christ healed the sick. The ill and infirm came to Him and He healed all He touched. This put faith in my heart. I became hopeful that He might heal me, too.

Christ gave peace to the troubled. He urged, "Have faith in God! Don't be troubled! There is no reason to fear!" Christ hated fear, showing man that he was born to live by faith. Christ gave confidence, faith and peace to those who came to receive help. This tremendously powerful message thrilled my heart.

Christ raised the dead. I never found one incident in the Bible where Christ conducted a funeral service. He brought the dead to life, changing funeral services into magnificent resurrections.

Most outstanding in my mind was Christ's mercy to the demon possessed. During the Korean War, many people lost their families and businesses. Suffering from nervous breakdowns, many became completely possessed by the devil. Bereft of shelter, they wandered aimlessly around on the streets.

Christ was even ready to meet this challenge. He cast out demons and restored the possessed to a life of normalcy. Christ's love was powerful, touching the lives and needs of all who came to Him.

Convinced that Jesus Christ was alive and moved by the vitality of His ministry, I knelt down. I asked Christ to come into my heart, to save and heal and deliver me from death.

Instantly, the joy of salvation and the peace of Christ's forgiveness surged over me. I knew that I was saved. I was filled with the Holy Spirit too, and I stood up and shouted, "Glory be to the Lord!"

From that time, I read the Bible like a starving man eats bread. The Bible supplied the foundation for all the faith I needed. Despite the prognosis and old feelings of fear, I soon knew I was going to live. Instead of dying in three months, I was out of my death bed in six.

Since then, I began to preach the dynamic gospel of the Lord Jesus Christ. The girl whose name I never knew, taught me the most precious name I will ever know.

Through the years God had helped me to understand several important principles of faith. These are the principles I share with you in the chapters that follow, in order that you can enter into a higher dimension of faith and more abundant life with Jesus Christ.

Christ is unchanging. He is the same yesterday, today and forever!

Christ wants to bear your burdens. He can forgive and heal you. He can cast out Satan and give you confidence, faith and peace.

Christ wants to give you life eternal and be a present part of your daily living. While thieves come to kill and destroy, Jesus Christ comes to give you life, life full and free.

Through the presence of the Holy Spirit, Jesus is with you right now. Christ desires to heal you and to deliver you from death. He is your living Lord. Put your faith in Jesus Christ, and expect a miracle today.

1

Incubation: A Law of Faith

God demonstrates His great power through you and your personal faith.

The Bible says, "God hath dealt to every man the measure of faith." (Romans 12:3) So it is taken for granted that you do have faith, whether you feel it or not. You may try to "feel" faith: but whether you feel it or not, when you need faith, it is there.

It is there for you to use. You have two arms. When you need to use them you just reach out your arms and move them. You don't need to feel that they are hanging from your shoulders in order to know that you have them.

There are, however, certain ways your faith works and links you to the heavenly Father who dwells within you. The Bible says that faith is the "substance of things hoped for," a substance which first has a stage of development— of incubation—before its usage can be full and effective. You may ask now, "What are the elements needed to make my faith usable?" There are four basic steps to the process of incubation.

Principle of Looking Ahead (Clear-cut Objectives)

First, to use your faith you must be able to envision a clear-cut objective. Faith is the substance of "things (clear-cut things) hoped for." If you have a goal but if it is vague and not fully defined, you are out of touch with the One Who can fulfill your goal because you are not sure yourself exactly what your goal is. You must have a clearly defined faith goal to experience faith to work for you. I learned this lesson from a very peculiar incident.

I had been in the ministry for quite a few months and was so poverty-stricken that, as far as material things were concerned, I had nothing. I was not married and I was living in one small rented room. I had no desk, no chair and no bed. I was eating on the floor, sleeping on the floor and studying on the floor yet walking miles and miles everyday to carry out soul winning.

But one day while reading my Bible, I was tremendously impressed by God's promises. The Bible said that if I would just put my faith in Jesus, praying in His name, I would receive anything I asked for. The Bible also taught me that I was a son of God, a child of the King of kings, and the Lord of lords!

So I said, "Father, why should a child of the King of kings, and the Lord of lords live without a desk, chair and bed and also walk mile after mile every day? At least I should have a humble desk and a chair to sit on and a humble bicycle to ride on to do my home visitation." I felt that according to the Scripture, I could ask for these kinds of things from the Lord. I knelt down and prayed, "Father, now I am praying. Please send me a desk, a chair and a bicycle." I believed and praised God for the things I had asked for.

From that moment on I waited for the delivery of each thing I had prayed for. A month passed with no answer. Then two months, three, four, five, six and I was still waiting. Nothing happened. Then one rainy day I was really depressed. Not having any food that evening, I was so hungry and tired that I started complaining, "Lord, I asked you to supply me with a desk, a chair and a bicycle several months ago but I have not received any of those things. You know that I am preaching the gospel to the poverty-stricken people of this slum area. How can I ask them to exercise faith when I cannot even practice it myself? How can I ask them to put their faith in the Lord and truly live by the Word and not by bread alone?"

"My Father, I am very discouraged. I am not sure about this, but I do know I cannot deny Your Word. The Word must stand. And I am sure that you are going to answer me, but this time I'm just not sure when or how. If you are going to answer my prayer after my death, what kind of profit will that have for me? If you are ever going to answer my prayer, please speed it up. Please!"

Then I sat down and began to cry. Suddenly, I felt a serenity and a feeling of tranquility came into my soul. Whenever I have that kind of feeling, a sense of the presence of God, He always speaks into my spirit so I waited. Then that still small voice welled up in my soul and the Spirit said, "My son, I heard your prayer long time ago."

Right away I blurted out, "Then where are my desk, chair and bicycle?"

Then the Spirit said, "You and all of my children beg me, demanding every kind of request but they ask in vague terms and that is why I do not answer. Don't you know that there are dozens of kinds of desks, chairs, and bicycles? You simply asked for a desk, a chair and a bicycle. You did not ask for a specific desk, a specific chair and a specific bicycle."

That was one turning point in my life. No professor in the Bible college ever taught me along these lines. I had made a mistake but it was an eye opener for me.

Then I said, "Lord, do you really want me to pray in definite terms?"

This time the Lord led me to turn to Hebrews the eleventh chapter, "Faith is the substance of things(clear-cut things) hoped for."

I knelt down to pray again. "Father, I am sorry. I made a great mistake. I misunderstood you. I cancel all my past prayers. I'll start all over again."

This time I gave Him the size of the desk that I would like and that it was to be made of Philippine mahogany. I wanted the best kind of chair, one made with an iron frame with rollers on the tips so that when I sat on it I could push myself around like a big shot.

Then I came to the bicycle and I really gave much consideration to the matter because there were so many kinds of bicycles: Korean, Japanese, Formosan and German. In those days, bicycles made in Korea or Japan were quite flimsy. I wanted to have a very strong sturdy bicycle; and since any machine made in the United States was the best, I said, "Father, I want to have a bicycle made in the United States with gears on the side so that I can even regulate the speed."

I ordered these things in such articulate terms that God could not possibly make a mistake in delivering them. Then I felt faith flowing up and out of my heart. I was rejoicing in the Lord and that night I slept like a baby.

But when I awoke at 4:30 a.m. to prepare for the early morning prayer meeting, I suddenly found that my heart was empty! The evening before, I had all the faith in the world, but while I slept it seemed that faith took wings and left me. I could not feel anything in my heart. I said, "Father, this is terrible. It is one thing to have faith but it is entirely different to keep that faith till I receive your answer."

This is a problem that is common to all Christians. They hear a special guest preacher and they are filled with faith while he is ministering to them but before they reach their homes, they have lost it all. It seems like their faith took wings and fled away, too.

That morning, while I was reading my Bible, looking for a particular scripture to speak on during early morning prayer meeting, suddenly my eyes fell on Romans 4:17, "God quickeneth the dead, and calleth those things which be not as though they were." My heart fastened itself to that scripture and the truth began to stir my heart. I said to myself, "I might as well just call those things which are not as if they were,—as if I already had them. I had received the answer to the problem of how to keep one's faith!"

I rushed out to our tent church where the people had already begun praying, and after a few songs I started preaching. I expounded that scripture and then said, "Folks, by the blessings of God, I have a desk made of Philippine mahogany, a beautiful chair with an iron frame and rollers on the tips, and a bicycle made in the United States that has gears on the side. Praise God, I've received all these things!"

The people just gasped because they knew that I was absolutely poverty-stricken. I was bragging about these things and they could not believe their ears. In faith, I was really praising God, doing just as the Word of God told me to do.

After the service, as I walked out, three young fellows followed me and said, "Pastor, we want to see those things."

I was taken aback and became frightened. I had not counted on having to show any of those things. These people were living in a slum area and once they knew I had lied, it would be my last time to minister there. They would never come back. I was in a terrible situation so I began to pray to the Lord: "Lord, from the beginning this wasn't my idea. It was your idea for me to tell it like that. I just obeyed you, and now I'm in a terrible situation. I spoke as if I have those things and now how can I explain this? You've got to always help me!"

Then the Lord came and helped me with an idea. I said, "You come to my room and see."

They all came and they looked around to see the desk, chair and bicycle. I said, "Don't look around. I'll show you later."

I pointed my finger at Mr. Park, who is now a pastor of one of the largest Assemblies of God churches in Korea and said, "I'll ask you a few questions. If you answer them, I'll show you all of those things. How long were you in your mother's womb before you were born?"

He scratched his head and said, "Well, nine months."

Then I asked again, "What were you doing for nine months in your mother's womb?"

"Oh, I was growing."

"But," I continued, "No one saw you."

"No one could see me because I was inside my mother."

Then I added, "You were as much a baby inside your mother's womb as you were when you were born into the world. You gave me the right answer. Last evening, I knelt down right here and prayed for that desk, chair and bicycle and by the power of the Holy Spirit, I conceived them. It is as if they are inside of me growing right now. And they are as much a desk, a chair and a bicycle as they will be when they are seen by people at the time of their delivery."

They started laughing and laughing. They said, "This is the first time we've ever seen a man pregnant with a desk, a chair and a bicycle." Then, rushing out of my room they began to spread the rumor all over town that the minister was pregnant with a desk, a chair and a bicycle. I could hardly walk through town without women gathering to look at me and giggle. Mischievous youngsters would come to me on Sunday, touch my stomach and say, "Pastor, look how big you are becoming! "

During those days, I knew every one of those things were growing in me. Just as it takes time for a mother to give birth to a child, it takes time for clear-cut objectives to come into reality for you.

I continued to praise the Lord every day for the things I had asked for and sure enough when God's time came, I had every one of those things. I had exactly what I had asked for—a desk made out of Philippine mahogany, a chair made by the Japanese Mitsubishi Company with rollers on the tips so that I could roll around when I sat on it, and a slightly used bicycle with gears on the side, from a missionary's son. I brought the desk, chair and bicycle home and my entire prayer life changed! God had taught me a tremendous truth.

Until this experience I had always prayed in vague terms, but from that time until today I never prayed in vague terms any more. If God ever answered vague prayers you would never recognize the vague prayer had been answered. For this reason the Word of God specifically states, "What things (be specific...) soever ye desire, when ye pray, believe that ye receive them, and ye shall have them." (Mark 11:24) You must ask definitely and specifically.

When the son of Timaeus, the blind Bartimaeus, came running after Jesus Christ, he cried, "Oh thou Son of David, be merciful to me." Although everybody knew that Bartimaeus was asking for the healing of his blindness, Christ asked, "What do you want me to do for you?" Christ wanted specific requests. Bartimaeus said, "Sir, I want to see." Jesus replied, "It shall be done unto you as you believe," and Bartimaeus' eyes were opened! Christ did not pronounce healing before Bartimaeus specifically asked for healing. When you bring your request to the Lord, come with a specific request, a definite objective, a clear-cut goal that you desire to see accomplished.

Once, when I was the visiting preacher in a church, the pastor's wife invited me to the pastor's office. There the pastor asked me to pray for a lady.

"For what shall I pray?" I asked.

"Well, she wants to get married and she still hasn't found an eligible person."

"Ask her to come in," I said.

A nice spinster who was over thirty years old, walked in. "Sister, how long have you been praying for a husband?" I asked.

"For more than ten years," she answered.

"Why hasn't God answer your prayer for more than ten years?" I asked. "What kind of husband have you been asking for?"

She shrugged her shoulders, "Well, that's up to God. God knows all."

"That's your mistake," I said. "God works through your request. God is the eternal Source, but He works through your specific requests. Do you really want me to pray for you?"

"Yes."

"Okay, bring me some white paper and a pencil and sit down in front of me." She sat down and I began, "If you write down the answers to my questions, I'll pray for you. Number one: Now you really want a husband but what kind of husband do you want? Asian, Caucasian, or Black?"

"Caucasian."

"Okay. Write it down. Now, number two: Do you want your husband to be as tall as six feet or as short as five feet?"

"Oh, I want to have a tall husband."

"Write that down. Number three: Do you want your husband to be slim and nice looking or just pleasantly plump?"

"I want him to be skinny."

"Write down skinny. Number four: What kind of hobby do you want your husband to have?"

"Well, musical."

"Okay, write down musical. Number five: What kind of job do you want your husband to have?"

"School teacher."

"Okay, write down school teacher." I went through ten points with her, and then said, "Please read aloud your list." So she read each point one through ten aloud. Then I said, "Close your eyes. Can you see your husband now?"

"Yes, I can see him clearly."

"Okay, let's order him now. Until you see your husband clearly in your imagination you cannot order specifically. If you are not specific, how would you know when God would answer? You must see him clearly before you begin to pray. In other words you must be specific in your request before you pray because God does not answer vague prayers that you yourself are not sure of."

So she knelt down and I laid my hands on her and prayed, "Oh God, now she knows specifically what kind of husband she would like. I see her husband by faith. You know her husband. We order him in the name of Jesus Christ."

"Sister, take this written paper to your home and paste it on a mirror. Every evening before you go to sleep read those ten points aloud, and every morning when you get up, read those ten points aloud, and praise God for the answer."

One year passed and I was passing through that area again. The wife of the minister called me on the telephone. She said, "Pastor, would you please come and have lunch with us?"

"Of course I will," I said. So I went to have lunch with them.

As soon as I arrived at the cafeteria she said, "Oh, she got married! She got married!"

"Who got married?"

"Do you remember that girl you prayed for? You asked her to write down those ten points? She got married!"

"Yes," I said. "Now, I remember. What happened?"

"That particular summer at the church one high school

music teacher came in with a quartet, staying in that church for a one-week singing revival. He was a single man and all of the young girls were crazy about him; they wanted to date him, but this guy was nonchalant to the young girls. Yet he was fascinated with the older spinster. He was always hanging around her and before he left, he asked her to marry him. Eventually she, not so reluctantly, gave her consent.

"So they got married in that church, and on their wedding day, her mother took that paper written with the ten points and read it publicly before the people and then tore it up."

It may sound like a fairy tale but it is true. It really works like that. I want to remind you of one thing: God is within you. He never works anything independently of you that concerns your life. He wants to work through your thinking, your faith and your clearly defined requests. So, whenever you want to receive answers from the Lord, place a clear-cut objective before Him specifically in prayer.

Do not just say, "Oh God, bless me, bless me!" Do you know how many blessings the Bible has? There are 8,000 promises. If you say, "Oh God, bless me," then God would ask you, "Out of the 8,000 promises, what kind of blessing do you want?" Though He knows your heart, the Bible says you must ask: "Ask and it shall be given you..." (Matt. 7:7) and this includes asking specifically. So be very definite. Take out your notebook, write it down, and see it clearly.

I always ask God to give a revival to my church and I ask according to a definite number. In 1960, I began to pray, "God, give us one thousand more members each year." And until 1969, one thousand members were added to my church each and every year.

But in 1969 I changed my mind and thought, "If God could give one thousand members per year, why shouldn't I ask God to give one thousand members per month?"

So since 1979 I started praying, "Father, give us one thousand members per month."

At first God gave 600, then began to give more than 1,000 per month. In one year, we received 12,000 new members in our church. Then I increased my goal and we had 15,000 additional members by the end of that year. The following year I asked for 20,000 more members. If you have a definite request you want to place before the Lord in prayer, if you can really see it, then you will have faith to receive it.

When I was building the present church structure which seated 10,000 in the first phase, even before they poured the concrete, I saw it clearly by the eyes of my heart. I walked hundreds of times in that building, and I felt the magnificent presence of the Holy Spirit there. I felt the magnitude of that church and it was a thrill to my heart. You must see your objective, your request, so vividly and graphically that you can really feel it in your heart! If you do not exercise this law of faith you can really never have the faith to receive an answer for the things you requested.

Now when I pray, I always try to envision a clear-cut objective. I want to see my objective so vividly that I feel a thrill in my heart when I pray. It is then that this first condition is completed.

Have a Burning Desire

Secondly, now that you have a vivid picture, you then should have a burning desire to receive those objectives. Many people pray casually, "God, answer my prayer," and before walking out of the church they have forgotten all the things they prayed for. This kind of attitude will never bring the faith and the touch of God. You need to have a burning desire.

Proverbs 10:24 reads, "The desire of the righteous shall be granted." Psalm 37:4 says, "Delight thyself also in the Lord; and he shall give thee the desires of thine heart." How much do you desire to have your request granted? You should have a burning desire for the petition accomplished. When I started my ministry in 1958, I had a burning desire in my soul to build the largest church in Korea. It was a goal that I desired so much that it burned in my soul. It was burning in me so steadily that I was living with it, sleeping with it and walking with it all the time. Today, it is said that my church is the largest church in the world.

It is necessary to have a burning desire in your heart to see your goal or objective fulfilled. If you do not have such a desire, then you should wait before God in prayer and ask Him to impart His desire in your heart so that you will have a fervent desire. From the Scripture we learn that God does not like a lukewarm heart. He specializes in great answers to a prayer when one has a fervent desire to experience His working. When you have a red-hot burning desire for the request or goal you pray for, you are going to have results.

Pray for Assurance

Third, you must have the substance or assurance. "Substance" in the Greek language is "hupostasis." In the English language this can be translated "title deed" or "legal paper." When a goal is clearly defined in your heart and you have such a burning desire in your heart to a boiling point, then you should pray until you receive the "substance," the assurance.

When I was conducting a meeting in Hawaii, a Japanese woman came to me and asked how long she should pray to receive assurance. I told her that sometimes it takes only a minute. If she should have peace and assurance in her heart in that minute, she would not need to pray any longer. "But," I said to her, "it could sometimes take two minutes, two hours, two weeks, two months, or two years; but whatever the length of time, you should pray until you pray through and you know you have this assurance."

Westerners are often wrapped up in the problem of trying to live according to schedules. Their lives are full of rush, rush, rush. When this happens, they soon start losing the time to have fellowship with family and friends, and even time to wait upon the Lord. They want everything instantly: instant breakfasts, T.V. dinners, fast food counters. Everything must be ready in five minutes. When they go to church they seem to pray, "Oh God answer me quickly. I have no time—five minutes—and if you are not going to answer me quickly, forget about it." They are not waiting upon the Lord.

Americans have often turned churches into a place for lengthy entertainment. In Korea, we have gotten rid of entertainment in the church. Announcements are very short and the Word of God takes preeminence. After preaching the Word, we may have a few special songs and corporate prayer and then we conclude. But the Word of God is always uppermost.

I had been invited to speak in an evening service in a church in Alabama. The service began at seven o'clock and the announcements and musical preliminaries took almost two hours. I got sleepy just sitting there. The people also began to feel tired, and then the presider came to me and said, "Cho, please speak only ten minutes tonight. We have a wonderful television show coming on tonight so I want you to preach for only ten minutes." I had come all the way from Korea by his invitation to speak only ten minutes that evening.

In such a church you cannot have the full blessings of the Lord. In a church there needs to be the time of waiting upon the Lord, praise and worship as well as a solid preaching of the Word of God. That builds faith. And you must have time to wait upon the Lord to receive the full assurance.

Before we began to build our present sanctuary, I felt the Lord had placed a burning desire in my heart to build this church which would seat 10,000 people. But when we needed five million dollars to build the church, already under contract, my heart was full of fear. I was shaky, fearful and I did not have the complete assurance. I was like a frightened rabbit and that five million dollars looked like Mount Everest. To rich foreigners a million dollars may mean relatively little; but to Koreans a million dollars means a great deal of money. So I began to pray like a dying person. I said, "Lord, now they've started the construction. But still I have no assurance. I don't know where we can get all this money."

I began travailing. A month passed and still no peace or no assurance. Another month passed and I was praying into the middle of every night. I would roll out of bed and go to the corner of my room and cry, sobbing my heart out. My wife thought that I was losing my mind, but I was mentally blinded. I would just stand without thinking, worrying about that five million dollars.

I prayed incessantly like that for three months. One morning my wife called, "Honey, breakfast is ready." As I was walking out of my study, just about to sit in my chair, suddenly the heavens opened up and the tremendous blessings of the Lord poured into my heart! And this great title deed, the substance and the assurance, was imparted into my soul. Suddenly I jumped out of my chair as if I had been shot and I began to shout, "I've got it! I've got it! Oh, I've got it!"

My wife rushed out of the kitchen and when I looked at her I saw that her face was absolutely pale. She was frightened, and holding me, said, "Honey, what's happened to you? Are you all right? Sit down."

"I've got it! " I replied.

"What do you have?"

"I have five million dollars," I strongly asserted.

Then she said, "You are really crazy now, really crazy."

"But Honey, I've got all these five million dollars inside of me. They're growing now! Oh, inside me they are growing!" Suddenly those five million dollars seemed to turn into a small pebble in the palm of my hand. I had prayed with assurance. My faith had reached out, and I had grabbed hold of that five million dollars; it was mine. The burning desire caused me to pray UNTIL I had the "substance,"—the assurance that the funds I needed would come.

I got the "substance," and once you have the substance, the title deed, or the legal paper, whether you see those things or not, legally those things are bound to come to you because legally those things belong to you. So pray through—pray until you have this assurance.

As I was praying the early part of the year 1991, God gave me the assurance of a total of 700,000 members in my church. So I claimed it, and in my heart I saw those 700,000 members. The fulfillment of this vision and assurance were inside me growing and as the vision grew inside of me, the same number of new believers was growing outside. This is the secret: pray until you get the substance and assurance.

Speak the Word

Fourth, you should show evidence of your faith. The Bible says that God raised the dead. It means that God performed miracles, calling "those things which be not as if they were."

When Abram was seventy-five years old, God told him to leave his country and promised that He would give the land of Canaan to his offspring. But Abram and Sara had no son. God gave them a promise for a son and when they received the assurance of that promise, God changed their names: "You are no more Abram, but Abraham, the father of many nations; and you should not call your wife Sara, but Sarah, the princess." This happened when Abraham was ninety-nine years old.

Abraham may have protested to God, "Father, people will laugh at us. We don't even have a puppy in our home and you mean you want us to change our names to 'the father of many nations,' and 'the princess?' My, all the people in town will call us crazy!"

But God may have said,"If you want to work with me you should do as I do: I call those things which be not as if they were. If you don't speak the word by faith as if you had already received the son, then you will not receive a son from me."

So Abraham changed his name. He came to his wife and said, "Dear, now my name is changed. I am no more Abram but Abraham, 'the father of many nations,' for God changed my name. Your name is no more Sara but 'Sarah.'"

One evening, Abraham was working far down in the valley. Sarah had prepared a meal and she called to her husband, "Abraham, the supper is ready." Those new names reverberated throughout all of the village.

People in the village probably stopped working and said, "Listen! She's calling her husband Abraham, 'the father of many nations!' Oh, poor Sara! She wanted to have a child so badly in her ninetieth year that she's started calling her husband 'the father of many nations!' She's lost her mind. Oh, we feel sorry for her."

Then suddenly they heard a big baritone sound from the valley. "Sarah, I'm coming."

"What!" they probably thought with surprise, "Sarah, 'the princess, the mother of many children?' Oh, he's in the same boat! They're both crazy."

But Abraham and Sarah ignored the criticism of the

villagers. They called each other: "the father of many nations," and "the princess." And exactly as they addressed each other, exactly as they gave affirmation, one day they had a beautiful child, Isaac, whose name means "smile."

Brothers and sisters, would you like to see a smile? Would you like to see smiles in your home? Would you like to have the people in your businesses and churches smile? Use the language of faith! Then you can see the birth of your "Isaac" again and again in your life.

Miracles do not come by struggling blindly. There are laws in the spiritual realm you can use too. And you have endless resources in your heart. God is dwelling within you by the Holy Spirit and He wants to do wonderful things for you when you speak the words of faith. God will help you accomplish great things. God is the same, for Jehovah never changes, but He will not manifest himself to a person until the person changes his language and speaks the word of faith. God used Moses and Joshua and other men of great faith; but when they passed away and the Israelites backslid, God stopped manifesting His power.

Today, God wants to manifest Himself through you just as He did through Christ 2,000 years ago. He is still as powerful as He has always been and He has a plan to use you. I believe that I could very easily build a church which has more than 10,000 people in the States, in Germany, or in Japan for when the Holy Spirit births a vision, that vision for a church is not built in the external world first but inside the heart of a man or a woman first through his faith.

Whatever is birthed by the Spirit into your heart and mind will also become impregnated in your heart and mind to be birthed into your circumstances. Watch your heart and mind carefully more than anything else. Do not try to find the answer of God through another person. God wants His answer to come to you instead of through another person. And through your spirit that answer will come into your circumstances.

When that word comes, claim the word of assurance and then speak it, for your spoken word of faith actually goes forth to create what you have spoken. God spoke and the whole world came into being. Your word of faith is the material which the Holy Spirit will use to create what you have requested.

So speak the word for this is very important. The church today has lost the art of giving commands. We Christians are becoming perennial beggars, for we are constantly begging. On the bank of the Red Sea Moses begged, "Oh God, help us! The Egyptians are coming." God rebuked him saying, "Moses, why are you crying to me? Give the command and the Red Sea shall be divided."

There are times for you to pray, but there are also times for you to give the command. You must pray through in your prayer closet first; but when you come out to the battlefield, you are coming to give the word of creation so you must command with authority that thing to happen. When we read the life of Jesus Christ, we see that He always gave commands. He prayed all night, but when He came out to the front lines He commanded that the people be healed. He commanded the sea to be calm. He commanded the devil to leave.

And His disciples did exactly the same things. To the beggar, Peter commanded: "Silver and gold have I none, but what I have, give I unto you. Rise up in the name of Jesus Christ!" To the body of a dead woman, Peter commanded: "Dorcas, rise up!" To the cripple at Lystra Paul commanded: "Stand on your feet!" With authority, they spoke the word of creation and Dorcas rose and the crippled man walked!

The Bible commands us to heal the sick. Of course it is through the Christ's life in us. In James the Bible says, "The prayer of faith shall save the sick." God clearly asks us to speak in faith and heal the sick; so in my church the sick are healed as the Holy Spirit guides me. I simply stand before them and claim, "You are healed! Stand up!" I call out different healings and people receive healing by the dozens or by the hundreds.

Several years ago, I was holding a meeting in a western country. One evening we had about 1,500 people packed into this one place, and right in front of me was one lady in a wheelchair. She was so badly twisted that I felt depressed. I asked, "Lord, why did you put her in front of me? When I see her, I can't exercise faith." So I tried to avoid looking at her while I was preaching. I would look one way, and then suddenly turn around and look the other way; for the sight of her seemed to pour cold water on my heart.

At the close of the service the Holy Spirit suddenly spoke into my heart, "Walk down and lift her up."

I replied, "Dear Spirit, you really mean that I should go down and lift her up? She is so twisted, I wonder if Jesus Christ Himself could lift her up. I can't do that. I am scared," and I struggled to obey.

But the Holy Spirit said, "You go and lift her up."

I still refused, saying, "Oh, no, I'm afraid."

So I started calling out the types of healing that the Holy Spirit showed me taking place in people except that woman. First a blind lady was healed. She was so frightened when I called out her healing she shrieked and fainted, just after her eyes had suddenly opened. Then people began to be healed all over the auditorium. I kept calling out healing continuously but the Holy Spirit kept saying to me, "Go down and lift her up."

I replied again, "Father, she is too twisted and I'm scared."

In the last moments of the service, I gave in, and when the pastor asked all the people to stand up and sing the concluding song, I slipped down and spoke with a whisper so people would not hear me, "Lady, if you wish, you could come out of that chair." Then I stood up and hurriedly walked away.

When I turned around all the people had started shouting and clapping their hands for that woman stepped out of her wheelchair and started walking around the platform. I was foolish, for if I had lifted her up in the beginning of that service as the Holy Spirit had instructed me to, heaven would have come down in that meeting that night.

Many people come and ask me whether I have the gift of faith or the gift of healing. I've searched my heart but so far I have not found any gift in me. I believe the Holy Spirit has all nine of the gifts and since He dwells within me, when a manifestation of any of the gifts is needed and I am available, it is He that manifests Himself through me. I only have the Holy Spirit and I just obey and believe in Him.

What kind of gift do I have? I will tell you the one gift I have—the gift of boldness. With this gift, one just launches out by faith; being led by the Holy Spirit. The Bible does not say that a sign shall go ahead of you; the Bible says that signs shall "follow" you. You must go forward for the signs to follow you. Abide by the law of "incubation," and throughout your life you will note that sign after sign will follow your path of faith.

All the resources of the Holy Spirit are within you since He indwells your life. Now, you know the elements of faith you need to enable your faith to translate into action. Understand that you must have a clear-cut goal and objective. Make it as clear as possible in your heart. Have a burning desire to see it fulfilled and then pray until you have the "substance," the assurance that it is beginning to take place. Then speak about your goal with words of assurance until your faith becomes sight!

2

The Fourth Dimension

Just as there are certain steps that we must follow in order for our faith to be properly incubated, there is also a central truth concerning the nature of faith's realm that we need to understand. The most important lessons that I have learned about the nature of the realm of faith began as a result of what was at first an unpleasant experience.

In America, ministers do not have this kind of problem, but in the Orient I have often experienced a problem in preaching about the miraculous power of God. That is because in Buddhism, monks also perform fantastic miracles. Years ago, one woman in Korea was dying of cancer. No doctor could cure her. She went to many churches and then to a Buddhist monk. He took her to a grotto where many people were praying, and there she was completely healed and cleansed and the cancer disappeared.

In Korea, many people who are involved in yoga heal the sick by yoga meditation. When people attend meetings of the Japanese Sokagakkai, many are healed of stomach ulcers; the deaf and dumb hear and speak, and the blind see. So, naturally we Christians, especially Pentecostal Christians, have real difficulty in explaining these occurrences. You cannot put these things away simply as a manifestation of the devil. But if the devil could do these things, why shouldn't the Church of Jesus Christ bring healing to the sick even more?

I was quite troubled one day, for many of our Christians were not considering God's miracles to be of importance. They said, "Oh, how can we believe in God as the absolute Supreme Being? How can we call Jehovah God the unique Creator in heavenly places? We see miracles in Buddhism, miracles in yoga and miracles in Sokagakkai. We see many miracles in the Oriental religions. Why should we claim Jehovah God as the only Creator of the universe?"

But I knew that our God is the supreme God, the only God and the Creator of the universe. I just did not know how to explain the happenings to my people. So I made their questions a matter of prayer. I fasted and prayed, seeking the Lord for answers. Then a glorious revelation came to my heart and I received a clear explanation. From that time on, I have explained these things to my people through my preaching in my church. Now, I feel I can give a satisfactory reply to any of those questions. Let me explain it to you.

In the universe there are three forces at work: the Holy Spirit of God, the spirit of Satan and the human spirit of man.

In the study of geometry, you can put up two points, one here and one there and if you draw an axis passing through those two points, you have created a space of "one dimension." If you add another axis which intersects the first one, you have created a space of "two dimensions"—or a plane. If you add another axis which intersects the first two at one point, you have created a space of "three dimensions"—or a cube. The first dimensional space, a line, is contained in and therefore controlled by the two dimensional space, a plane; the two dimensional space is contained and controlled by the three dimensional space, a cube. Using the metaphor of geometry and its dimensions we can compare the material and physical world.

Our material and physical world belongs to the three dimensional space. But who controls this world of three dimensions? There is a world of four dimensions. Then what is the fourth dimension? You have a revelation of this in Genesis 1:2, "And the earth was without form, and void; and darkness was upon the face of the deep. And the Spirit of God moved upon the face of the waters."

If you look into the original language of this scripture, you see it conveys the meaning that the Spirit of the Lord was "incubating" over the waters. He was brooding or hovering over the waters. Using the metaphor of the one, two, and three dimensional spaces, the chaotic world belonged to the three dimensional space and the Holy Spirit pictured here—incubating or "hovering over"— belongs to the higher dimensional realm where all of God's power is available and working.

The evil spirit world, the kingdom of darkness, which is controlled by Satan, belongs to a spirit realm with supernatural power but it is not the spiritual realm. Totally different from the realm of the Holy Spirit, counterfeits of healing and miracles can take place in the evil spirit realm, imitating the work and the power of God as the magicians of Egypt did. In this realm, a flair for unusual experiences may draw many followers. Satan's purpose is always to deceive unbelievers and to insist that they can have a religious experience without the born-again experience with Jesus Christ. Although the evil spirit world can counterfeit the power of God, its power and ability is still limited and it still comes under the power and the authority of Almighty God. It can never touch the higher dimensional realm of the Holy Spirit where eternal life changes are made!

Since the Holy Spirit hugged or hovered over the three dimensional realm, it was by this "incubation" of the four dimensional being on the three dimensions and God's spoken Word created the world. A new order was given out of the old and life came forth from death; beauty appeared from ugliness and void, cleanliness from things that were dirty and abundance from poverty!

Then God spoke to my heart, "Son, as the two dimensional space includes and controls the one dimensional space and the three dimensional space includes (or contains) and controls the two, so the four dimensional space contains and controls the three dimensional world producing the creation of order and beauty. Every human being is a physical being with the potential of being a spiritual being. Men and women without Christ are still dead in their sins and trespasses and cannot experience the Holy Spirit realm. They cannot live in the four dimensional realm of the Holy Spirit until they are born again and receive Christ. And man's spirit is joined to either the evil spirit world or the spiritual realm where the Holy Spirit leads, guides and enables him to be alive in Christ. Both the unsaved and the born again Christian explore their spiritual sphere of their own four dimensional world. Apart from God, man's unredeemed spirit can never have access to spiritual blessings or power. But he can try to commune with his four dimensional world by having clear-cut visions and actually experience some kind of spirit world that enables him to have a counterfeit of peace and serenity.

Often the best that these people can experience is some type of Eastern mysticism that borders close to demon possession.

With clear-cut visions and mental pictures of health,

they incubate over their bodies that belong to the three dimensional world. Since they take dominion over their human spirit, sickness and disease, they may have results.

The Sokagakkai belong to Satan. Their human spirit joins up with the evil fourth dimension too, and they take dominion over their bodies and circumstances. The Holy Spirit revealed to me that it was in this manner that the magicians in Egypt carried out dominion over various occurrences in which they competed with Moses.

God then taught me that since born again believers are joined to the Holy Spirit's four dimensional realm, to our heavenly Father, the Creator of the Universe, through our Lord Jesus Christ, we can take more dominion over our circumstances than the unsaved people. Praise God! We can become creative and can exercise control and power over the changing situations in the three dimensional world—all by the power of the Holy Spirit in us.

So the greatest difference between the two healings— in the Oriental religions and in the Christian churches—is that the Oriental religious leaders explore their own fourth dimension, open their lives to what they believe to be their spirit world. Healing may take place by their faith in it. But there is no living Christ that assures them of salvation nor a life with Jesus Christ throughout eternity.

Rather, many of these people live on the border of demon possession or have opened their lives to many evil spirits whose voices they hear and obey.

After receiving this revelation from the Lord, I began to easily explain the happenings and miracles of other religions. People would come to me and challenge me, "We can do the same miracles." Then I would say, "Yes, I know you can. It's because you have your own fourth dimension in your spirit. You are developing your spirit to take dominion over your body and circumstances; but that is not the spirit that has been born again by the blood of Jesus Christ with a knowledge of sins forgiven! You may have a certain limited amount of power over your body since you are linked to the evil fourth dimension. Only Christ has limitless power over all forces and power on earth!"

The Role of the Subconscious

In America, I find a lot of mind-expanding books and I see a lot of these teachings happening so many places because of all the emphasis on the subconscious. What is the subconscious? The subconscious is your spirit, the inner man, the hidden man of your heart.

The Apostle Paul had discovered subconscious almost 2,000 years before modern psychology did. Now scientists and psychologists make a great deal of this discovery, digging into the ideas of the subconscious and trying to direct its energies. Though the subconscious is in the four dimensional world with certain limited power, a great amount of deception is involved in what these people claim.

I was amazed when I came to America and read some of the books American pastors gave me because these books seemed to make the subconscious into an almighty god. That is a great deception. The subconscious has certain influence, but it is quite limited and it cannot create like our Almighty God can. I began to see the Unitarian Church in America trying to develop the subconscious, the fourth dimension of the human spirit, and put that human spirit in the place of Jesus Christ. This indeed is a great deception and a great danger. While we do recognize certain realities and truths in these teachings, it is also important to realize that the devil occupies an evil fourth dimension. God however is holy, unique, and almighty. The four dimensional realm is always creating and giving order, and taking dominion over the three dimensional world by means of incubation, but this is not true of Satan's four dimensional world.

Several years ago, I was watching the television news in the United States and there was a great controversy in one city over a murder case. The defense lawyer claimed that the young murderer had been intoxicated by violent television programs. There was a certain truth in that because the boy, after watching the television shows, began to connect to his fourth dimension. He began to think, "incubate," and meditate on those acts of violence and as a result, he hatched the same sin of murder.

The Language of the Fourth Dimension

My ministry has been revolutionized since I discovered the truth of the fourth dimension, and your life can be revolutionized by this truth too. You may wonder how we can incubate the three dimensions. We dwell in limited bodies, whereas the Holy Spirit in His omnipresence can simply incubate over the whole earth. But since we are so limited in space and time, the only way for us to incubate is through our imaginations, through the visions and dreams that the Holy Spirit has given us.

This is the reason the Holy Spirit comes to cooperate with us, to create, by helping young men to see visions and old men to dream dreams. Through looking ahead and dreaming dreams we can kick away the wall of limitations and we can stretch out to the universe. The Word of God says, "Where there is no vision, the people perish." (Prov. 29:18) While this pertains to having a vision for responsibility it can also apply to your purpose of life. If you have no vision, you are not being creative; and if you cease to be creative, you will soon lose your goals or purpose in life.

Visions and dreams are the languages of the fourth dimension. This is why the Holy Spirit placed many of them in your heart and continues to communicate to you through them. Through visions and dreams you can cooperate with the Holy Spirit to dream of bigger churches. You can look ahead a new mission field. You can look ahead the increase of your church. Through looking ahead the goals that you feel have been placed in your trust for God, you can incubate your future and hatch the results. So dream, and let the dreams develop into a desire to do great exploits for God. Meditate on them. Incubate them, and the Holy Spirit will work through you to bring them to pass. Let me substantiate this with some scriptural examples of another kind.

Do you know why Adam and Eve fell from grace? The devil knew that the four dimensional visions and dreams in the mind of a person could create a tremendous result. Using a tactic based on this premise, the devil invited Eve and said, "Eve, come over and look at the fruit on the forbidden tree. Looking at it is harmless so why don't you come over and just look at it?" So, since simply looking at the tree seemed to be harmless, Eve went and looked at the fruit of the tree. She looked at that tree not only once or twice, but she continued to look. The Bible says in Genesis 3:6, "And when the woman saw that the tree was good for food, she took of the fruit thereof, and did eat." Before she partook she saw the tree, also seeing this fruit in her imagination. She played with the idea of eating the forbidden fruit and brought that to her four dimensional world.

In the four dimensional world either good or evil is created. Eve brought that picture of the tree and fruit deep into her imagination, seeing the fruit clearly, imagining that it could make her as wise as God. Then she felt so attracted to that tree, it was as if she were being pulled toward it; next she took the fruit of the tree and ate, then gave some to her husband. And with that action they fell. Eve had been deceived by the serpent that she would not die but Adam ate willfully.

Seeing is very important! If it were not so, why did the angel of God give such a grievous judgement to Lot's wife? In Genesis 19:17 the Bible reads, "Escape for thy life; look not behind thee." It was a simple command: do not look behind you. However, when you read Genesis 19:26, you will discover that Lot's wife looked back and became a pillar of salt. She received the grievous judgement just because she looked back.

You might say that the judgement was too harsh, but when you understand this law of the spirit, it isn't; for when she looked back, she did not saw it with her physical eyes only. That sight came into her inner self and gripped hold of her imagination. Lust for her former life began to take hold of her, and the judgement of God was carried out.

God has been using this language of the Holy Spirit to change many lives. Look carefully when you read Genesis 13:14~15, "And the Lord said unto Abraham, after that Lot was separated from him, 'Lift up now thine eyes, and look from the place where thou art northward, and southward, and eastward, and westward: For all the land which thou seest, to thee will I give it, and to thy seed forever.'"

God did not say, "Oh Abraham, I'll give you Canaan. Just claim it." No. Very specifically, God told him to stand from his place, look northward, southward, eastward, and westward, and He would give that land to Abraham and his descendants.

Seeing is possessing. Abraham saw the land; he then

went back to his tent, and to his bed, to dream of the lands which were going to become his. In his four dimensional world, the Holy Spirit began to use that language. The Holy Spirit began to carry out dominion.

It is interesting that Abraham got Isaac when he was one hundred years old and Sarah was ninety. When Abraham was almost one hundred years of age and Sarah almost ninety, God spoke to them about the son and Abraham laughed and laughed. This means that Abraham was totally unbelieving.

We also see that Sarah laughed behind the tent. God asked, "Sarah, why are you laughing?" She replied, "I didn't laugh." But God said, "Yes, you did laugh."

Both Abraham and Sarah laughed. They were both unbelieving. But God had a way to make them believe. God used the fourth dimension and the language of the Holy Spirit. One night God said to Abraham, "Come out of your tent." In the Middle East the humidity is very low, so at night you can see many stars sparkling in the sky. Abraham went out and God said, "Abraham, count the number of the stars." So he started counting.

Scientists say that with the human eye we can count 6,000 stars. So we can imagine Abraham counted and counted until he eventually forgot the number. Finally he said, "Lord, I can't count all of them." Then the Lord said, "Your children are going to become as numerous as those stars!" Counting the vast number of stars was to help Abraham grasp the enormity of the miracle of God's promise!

I imagine that Abraham was struck with emotion. Tears probably welled up in his eyes and his vision probably became completely blurred. When he looked up at the stars, he probably envisioned the stars as the faces of his children who would be calling to him, "Father Abraham! Father Abraham!" He was all shaken up just thinking about his children. No doubt he was sleepless when he closed his eyes that night for he saw in his imagination all the stars changing into the faces of his descendents shouting, "Father Abraham."

Those scenes no doubt came to his mind again and again and became his own dreams and pictures in his heart. They immediately became part of his fourth dimension in the language of spiritual visions and dreams. They prepared his heart and carried dominion over his one-hundred-year-old body so that when God's Spirit made Abraham fertile, he and Sarah were prepared for their miracle. From that time on, he had a new faith in the Word of God and he praised the Lord!

What could change Abraham so greatly? It was the Holy Spirit, because God had applied the law of the fourth dimension, the language of the Holy Spirit. A vision and dream changed Abraham and he lived in that vision with faith and expectancy until his son was born. That same vision helped him to believe his physical body was changing too—and not only his body but his wife's also. They were wonderfully rejuvenated. Later on in the Bible you can read just how rejuvenated Sarah had become. King Abimelech tried to make Sarah his concubine. Ninety year old Sarah had been rejuvenated through the law and language of the fourth dimension as well as God's touch on their physical bodies!

We are not limited in our thinking like animals. When God created us, He created us with a spiritual fourth dimension so that when man receives Christ as His Savior, he is so transformed that he can live in his spiritual realm and understand the visions and dreams and work with the Holy Spirit to take dominion over his three dimensional world in which he lives and works.

I cannot carry out my ministry of winning souls by simply knocking on doors, struggling and working myself to death. I use the way of faith and the church is growing by leaps and bounds. And even though our church has more than 700,000 members, when I go to the office I do not have a great deal to do for I follow the path of faith. I am not constantly striving in my flesh to bring to pass those things that the Holy Spirit can easily do.

I learned that even while I minister in foreign countries I can go into the four dimensional realm of the Holy Spirit and tell Him what I feel is needed in my church and He carries out the work. I call my wife about every other day and she continually gives me information which at times has served as a blow to my ego. I used to think that the members of my church would be very anxious for my return from my trips abroad; they would be waiting for me, and I was sure that the Sunday service attendance would go down. She would say, "Don't brag about it. The church is doing well at all times even though you are not here."

Applying the Law of the Fourth Dimension

If God could enable Abraham to possess the land through the miraculous laws of the fourth dimension, and if God could rejuvenate Abraham and Sarah through the Holy Spirit's language of visions and dreams, then God will work for you in the fourth dimension of visions and dreams also.

There is a magnificent story about Jacob in Genesis 30:31~43. I had always disliked the portion of the scripture in verses 37 through 39 where Jacob made a plan to insure solid colored cattle would give birth to spotted and speckled cattle.

At first, this seemed like a superstition and I asked, "Lord, why do You permit this superstition in the Bible? This is one reason Modernists are criticizing the Bible, calling it a fairy tale."

So when I came to this part of the scripture, I would skip over it, fearing and worrying that there was a portion of the Bible I could not trust. One day while reading my Bible under the anointing of the Holy Spirit, I again came to these verses and said, "I'm going to skip this part. I'm not sure about this."

But the Holy Spirit said, "Wait a minute. Nothing in the Bible is a superstition. You just don't understand it. You are blind. I am applying the special law of creation here. Read this again."

Then an unveiling of truth came to me and this added

a new dimension to my ministry. If you do not use the miraculous laws of faith you cannot hope to see a thousand new members added to your church each month; your personal struggle apart from the working of the fourth dimension cannot bring this goal about.

During this time of his life, Jacob, whose name meant "the swindler," had gone to his Uncle Laban's home. He stayed for about twenty years, working hard as a common laborer for him. His uncle changed his salary many times and deceived Jacob. Then Jacob began to deceive his uncle also. They deceived each other. Although Jacob spent about twenty years with his uncle, he had nothing in the way of material gain—with a lot of wives and children—and he desired to return home.

God felt sorry for Jacob and showed him a portion of the secret of the fourth dimension. After receiving this revelation from the Lord, Jacob went to his uncle. "Uncle," he said, "I'll work for you on this condition: you take away all the spotted and speckled animals from me, and I'll tend only the animals with coats of solid colors. If in some way these solid colored animals give birth to spotted and speckled offspring, then those will become my salary."

Jacob's uncle probably thought to himself, "Oh, now this guy is cheating himself. Those solid colored animals have a very slim chance of giving birth to many spotted and speckled offspring. But it's his own plan so I will still use him without paying much salary."

Laban said to him, "Yes, yes. That's wonderful. I'll

make that contract with you."

Laban took all the spotted and speckled animals and removed them three days distance away, and Jacob was left with only the animals of solid color. Jacob went out to the mountain, cut down poplar, hazel and chestnut tree branches and with his pen knife made them all spotted and speckled. By placing them in the ground side by side he made a wall in front of the cattle's drinking trough, where the cattle would come for water and to conceive offspring.

There, Jacob would stand watching the animals in front of those spotted and speckled tree rods.

God had created a vision and dream in his mind. Before, his mind had been full of poverty, failure and cheating, so his struggle was hard and his reward was little. But God changed Jacob through the imagination of his mind by using a wall of spotted and speckled tree rods as material to help him see and dream. Jacob probably looked at that wall so much that his mind became filled with the sight. He probably dreamed of the cattle giving birth to spotted and speckled offspring. In the next chapter we read that the cattle did give birth to spotted and speckled offspring. (Genesis 30:39) Seeing with the eyes of your heart plays a great role in the four dimensional world. Animals don't have this ability because "seeing" is the work of the Spirit.

When Jacob began to grasp the vision and dream of spotted and speckled cattle, he began to learn the language of the Holy Spirit.

When he learned the language of the Holy Spirit, immediately he began to converse with the Holy Spirit and the Holy Spirit began to work. Today, we might say Jacob "saw by faith" what he could do and acted upon it. The Holy Spirit then punched the proper keys for the necessary genes, having the animals give birth to spotted and speckled offspring, something Jacob could not do. Jacob soon began to have vast flocks and herds of spotted and speckled animals, and he became one of the richest men in the Orient.

Long after Jacob lived, God put up another tree. This time it was a cross on Calvary. It was not spotted and speckled by a pen knife but by the real blood from the life of the Son of God. Anyone can come and gaze upon this tree, the cross of Jesus, and receive a new life, a new image, a new dream and vision by the power of the Holy Spirit, and be changed.

There are more than 8,000 promises in the Bible, and each one can be to you what the spotted and speckled tree was for Jacob. You do not need to go to the mountains to cut down a hazel, chestnut or a poplar tree. You can rather take the promises from the Bible, stained by the blood of Jesus and they will be the power of God to bring to pass the dream and vision that the Holy Spirit gave you.

Now let me share something from my personal experience with you. One Christmas Eve I was busy preparing a sermon. An urgent telephone call came in the early morning hours of Christmas day. It was from a doctor at

Seoul National University Hospital. He asked over the phone, "Is this Pastor Cho?"

"Yes, this is he."

"One of your members is dying here. He was in a car accident. A taxi driver hit him, then he drove around all through the night with him in the back seat."

In Korea at that time, if someone was hit and killed by a taxi, the taxi driver would only have to pay the sum of $2,500, and then he would be cleared of all financial obligation. However, if the victim survived with some injury, then the driver would have to pay all the medical and hospital bills. So, if a driver hit someone and no one saw the accident, he would drive that person around until he or she died. It would be cheaper for him.

This church member had just bought a beautiful hat and other gifts for his wife. He was so carried away with the joy of giving her these presents that he jay-walked across the street without observing the traffic light and was hit by a taxi. Since it was late in the evening and it seemed that no one saw the accident, this taxi driver carried the injured man in his car throughout the evening. The man did not die and eventually a policeman caught the taxi and took the injured man to a hospital. The impact of the accident had badly impaired the man's intestines. His stomach was full of dirt and blood, and blood poisoning had already set in.

His doctor knew me and called, saying, "Dr. Cho, should we operate on him? Medically speaking, it is hopeless. He was left without medical attention for such a long time and now blood poisoning has set in. There is nothing we can do."

But I said, "You go ahead and operate on him and as soon as I finish the Christmas sermon, I'll hurry to the hospital."

After the Christmas service I rushed to the emergency room of Seoul National University Hospital and there he was, totally unconscious. The doctor repeated again that there was no hope. "Reverend, don't expect anything. He is dying. We can do nothing. When we opened his abdomen, three areas of his intestines had been completely severed, and these areas were filled with excrement and dirt. There is no hope."

I replied, "Well, I'll try to do my best."

In his room, I knelt beside him and prayed: "Lord God, give me only five minutes. Let him come out of the coma for five minutes."

As I was praying I felt him moving. I opened my eyes and the man opened his eyes.

"Oh, Pastor, I'm dying," he cried.

Knowing that I had five minutes, I replied, "Don't say that. As long as you are saying you will die, you can't have faith. You must think of living through this ordeal. Change your thinking. The only way to take control over this three dimensional situation is through your faith, which will give you visions and dreams of being well again. Think wholeness!

"Listen to me. Picture a healthy young man saying

goodbye to his wife. He's in the full bloom of youth and health. He goes to his office and completes his business successfully. All the people respect and admire him. An evening arrives and he stops en-route home to purchase gifts for his wife. She's waiting for him to come home so that they can have dinner together. When he arrives, she rushes out to the gate and welcomes him with a big hug and a kiss. They go into the house and share a delicious meal together and a quiet evening at home.

"The man I am talking about is no stranger. That man is you! Think of that man! Draw that picture in your mind. Look at that man and say in your heart, 'I am that man!'"

"Don't draw a picture of death. Don't form a picture of a dead corpse. Keep on dreaming about that man, and I will do the praying. You just draw a mental picture and leave the praying to me. Will you do that?"

"Yes, pastor, I'll change my thinking. I'll believe that I am that man. I'll try to make that vision and dream a reality. I see it!" he cried.

While we were talking, the surgeon came in with his nurses. They started giggling and laughing at me. They probably thought I had lost my mind. But I was serious. I knew the law of the Spirit's fourth dimension and that man had begun to speak the language of the Holy Spirit. Like a missionary on a foreign field who gains a deeper level of communication with the local people of that country by learning to speak their language directly instead of using an interpreter, so that dying man had learned the deeper language of the Holy Spirit—to see himself completely well and believe it would happen.

As I knelt down and grabbed hold of his bed, I prayed, "Dear Holy Spirit, you are the Healer in the world today. Now he speaks your language. He has a vision and a dream of being completely healed and restored. Place your healing upon his physical body and take control. I command this man to be whole and to be filled with the healing power!"

Suddenly the group of unbelieving nurses said, "This room is hot. The heat is too high."

But the weather was not very cold outside. The room was not unreasonably hot. It was the power of the Holy Spirit at work healing this man. The surgeon and the nurses said they began to feel fire. Their ears turned red and the power of God became so strong that we even felt the bed trembling.

What happened? Both the sick man and I had released faith and the Holy Spirit worked in response to that faith. The Holy Spirit took control and healing took place! We spoke the language of the Holy Spirit and He manifested healing.

Amazingly, in one week, that man rose up and walked out of the hospital. He is now in the chemical business and doing wonderfully. Whenever I see him on Sunday mornings sitting in the balcony, I say to myself, "Praise God!" Because we spoke the same language as the Holy Spirit spoke, He created the healing! Hallelujah!

Let me tell you about another incident. One day I was

in my office when a lady about fifty years old came in crying that her home was completely broken and destroyed.

"Stop crying," I responded, "and tell me about it."

"You know we have several sons but only one daughter. She has become a hippie and she sleeps with my husband's friends and with friends of my sons. She goes from a hotel to another hotel and from this dance hall to that dance hall."

"She has become a shame to my family," she cried. "My husband cannot go to his office. My boys are dying of embarrassment and now they are all going to leave home. I've tried everything. I've even cried out to the Lord to strike her dead! Oh Pastor Cho, what can I do?"

"Stop whining and crying," I said to her. "Now I can see very clearly why God did not answer your prayer. You were presenting the wrong kind of mental blueprint to Him. In your mind you were always submitting the picture of a prostitute, weren't you? While pleading for the Holy Spirit to change her, you were dwelling on the negative and what was unacceptable to your own standard of life."

She retorted, "Well yes, that's what she is. She is a prostitute!"

"But if you want to see her changed, then you must submit another mental blueprint to the Holy Spirit when you pray," I said. "You must clean the canvas of your present imagination or image of her and you must start presenting a new picture of your daughter the way you know the Holy Spirit can change her."

But she was not listening to what I said. Instead, she responded with, "I can't. She's dirty, ugly and wretched." I began to perceive that she needed to forgive her daughter.

"Stop talking like that," I chided her. "Let's draw a new picture of your daughter. Kneel down here and I will kneel with you. Let's go to the foot of Calvary. Let's lift up our hands. Let's look at Jesus Christ dying on the cross, bleeding and beaten for all kinds of sins that mankind would commit.

"Why is He hanging there? Because of your daughter. Let's picture your daughter right behind Jesus Christ. Let's look at your daughter through His cross. Can't you see your daughter forgiven, cleansed, born again, and filled with the Holy Spirit—completely changed? Thanks to the blood of Jesus Christ that was shed for every one and every kind of sin, can you draw that picture of Jesus' forgiveness for your daughter?"

"Oh pastor, yes," the mother replied. "Now I see her differently. Through the cross of Jesus, now I can change my image of my daughter."

"Wonderful, wonderful!" I exclaimed. "Let's draw a new picture of your daughter, and then you keep that clear-cut vivid and graphic picture of a 'new' daughter in your mind day in and day out. That's seeing the same thing the Holy Spirit sees that your daughter will become. That's the language—the 'vision'—of the Holy Spirit. It's a positive vision of a cleansed and born again daughter.

That's how the Holy Spirit sees her now. Now, by faith, we will look at her the way the Holy Spirit does. We know we are drawing the right kind of picture since we are coming to the foot of the cross."

So we knelt down and prayed, "Oh Lord, now we see the picture of this daughter as you see her cleansed and changed. Now dear Holy Spirit, flow into this new image, this new vision and dream that you have birthed in our hearts. Change her! Perform miracles according to the vision."

As I sent the mother out she was all smiles. Crying had ceased for the image of her daughter had changed.

A few months later, on one Sunday, she suddenly walked into my office with a beautiful young lady.

"Who is this young lady?" I asked.

"This is my daughter," she said with a big smile.

"Did God answer your prayer?"

"Oh yes, He did," she replied.

Then she told me what had happened. One night her daughter had been sleeping in a hotel with a man. When she woke up in the morning, she felt dirty and wretched. She felt a great unhappiness in her spirit, and had a deep desire to return home but she was frightened and afraid. Nevertheless, she decided to risk her feelings and go home, saying to herself, "I'll try one more time and if they do not accept me, then that will be my last attempt to reconcile with my family."

She went home and rang the door bell. Her mother

came out, and seeing her daughter, her countenance lit up as if the sun was rising on her face.

"Welcome home, daughter," she greeted her and rushed out to hug her. Overwhelmed by her mother's love, the daughter crumbled into her mother's arms, crying.

During the next two or three months the daughter accompanied her mother to church. She listened to the sermons and soon she confessed her sins, surrendered her life to Jesus Christ and later received the baptism in the Holy Spirit. She became a new creation in Christ and eventually found a wonderful husband!

This is a touching story of the change that will come when we line up our thinking and speaking with the Holy Spirit's image of the completed work of Christ in our loved ones. This mother had begun to look upon her daughter as the Holy Spirit saw her: saved, filled with the Holy Spirit and living for God and her prayers were heard and answered.

Visions and dreams of what you and your family can become are born of the Holy Spirit into your heart in the first place, because these are the "language" of the Spirit. The Holy Spirit would reveal to you the picture of your prayer already answered; lives that have already been changed; circumstances already turned around and God receiving the glory for the work of redemption already effected in lives and situations we are praying for. As far as Jesus is concerned, the work is finished! The visions and dreams are to encourage you to see what He sees, as completed! This is living in the four dimensional realm—living and praying in the joy of the revelation the Holy Spirit gives, until you see it happen in actuality as this mother did.

This daughter now has three children of her own. She is a strong Christian and is one of the foremost fervent home cell unit leaders in my church. And all this was made possible because the mother changed her image of her daughter to the Holy Spirit's image of the daughter—applying the law of the fourth dimension.

Throughout the Scripture, God always used the law of the fourth dimension. Consider Joseph. Before he was sold as a slave, God had already imprinted in his heart the scenes of what would take place in his life one day. Through several dreams God gave Joseph a clear-cut vision. Though he was sold as a slave to the Egyptians, he was in control of his circumstances and believed that his dreams would come to pass. His dreams were prophetic promises to him from God. Though the Word of the Lord tried him, one day Joseph became the Prime Minister of Egypt.

Consider Moses. Before he built the tabernacle, God had called him to Mount Sinai. As he communed with God those forty days and nights he was given a picture of the exact design and plan for the tabernacle and he went and built it to the exact specifications by carrying out the visions that he had received in his heart and mind.

God gave visions to major prophets Isaiah, Jeremiah, Ezekiel and Daniel. God enabled them to see in the four dimensional realm, using the language of the Holy Spirit. Then they prayed with faith according to the revelation they received from the Holy Spirit.

This was true even of the Apostle Peter. His original name had been Simon. The meaning of the name Simon is "a reed," something that is bendable, changeable, and unpredictable. But when Andrew brought Peter to Jesus, Jesus looked upon him and said, "Yes, you are Simon—changeable and unpredictable like a reed—but now I am going to call you a rock because you are going to become a rock."

Simon, the 'reed' is dead to the world and now Peter the 'rock' is alive."

Since Peter was a fisherman, he knew the strong and stable qualities of a rock. In his imagination he immediately began to see himself portrayed as a rock. He would watch the wind-tossed waves of the Sea of Galilee splashing upon a rock, engulfing it with white foam; and the rock appeared to be conquered. But in the next moment he would see all the water breaking against the rock and returning to the sea, yet the rock stood still, unmoved. Peter thought, again and again, "Am I like a rock? Am I? Yes, I am like a rock." After Pentecost, Peter was baptized in the Holy Spirit and changed to become a strong pillar of the Early Church. Long before Peter was changed into this rock, Christ had seen a vision of Peter as a rock. Later Peter indeed became that rock. Jesus knew what Peter would become.

God knew that Jacob would become Israel, "the prince of God." Though he was a cheater and a swindler, God dealt with him until Jacob understood God's dealings in his life.   Then Jacob surrendered to God and later became "the prince of God."

Many non-Christians today from all over the world seem to be involved in transcendental meditation or Buddhistic meditation.   In meditation one is asked to have a clear-cut goal and vision during their act of meditation.   In Sokagakkai, one draws a picture of prosperity repeating phrases over and over, trying to develop the human spirit dimension; and these people achieve something.   While Christianity has been in Japan for more than 100 years, with only 0.5 percent of the population claiming to be Christians, Sokagakkai has millions of followers.   Sokagakkai applies the law of their fourth dimension and these followers perform some miracles; but in Christianity there seems to be only talks about theology and faith.

Our God is a God of miracles!   We, as His children, were created in the image of God and we were born with the desire to see miracles performed.   Without seeing miracles, people will not be willing to acknowledge that God is all powerful.   The great change in people is often evidence enough that God has performed the miracle of salvation to bring them from death into new life; nevertheless, people still want to see God reveal Himself in great power.

Your Responsibility

You and I are responsible to supply miracles for these people.

The Word declares, "Delight thyself also in the Lord; and He shall give thee the desires of thine heart." (Psalm 37:4) This is the key! Proverbs 10:24 reads, "The desire of the righteous shall be granted." God wants to give you the desires of your heart. He is ready to fulfill those desires.

The Bible is not of the three dimensions but of the four dimensions. In His Word we read about God and the life He has for us. Through the Word, we learn the language of the Holy Spirit—how the Holy Spirit can enlarge your visions and dreams and then fulfill them. Let Him do it. Let the Holy Spirit come and quicken the Scriptures you read. Let Him implant visions; and the desire of your heart shall be granted according to his Word, so that many people will behold the miracles that God has done for you and bring glory to God.

So, let the Holy Spirit teach you the language of the Holy Spirit, the language of dreams and visions. Then keep those visions. Keep those dreams. Cooperate with the Holy Spirit. Obey His leading in your life.

How do you do this? First, recognize a clear-cut goal in your heart in line with the desire of the Holy Spirit. Draw a mental picture of that goal vivid and graphic, praying fervently throughout the process. Do not be confused with the talk of "mind control," "mind expansion," yoga, transcendental meditation or Sokagakkai. These are cults and they are only developing the human fourth dimension, the evil fourth dimension of their spirit world.

Let us rise up and do more than any Egyptian magician could have done. There are plenty of these kinds of magicians in today's Egypt of this world. But let us receive all the visions and dreams that were birthed in our hearts by the Holy Spirit in the first place for our God. As God directed all the miracles using Moses and received all the glory, let us also, like Moses, know what God can and will do for us and allow the most wonderful miracles to come forth.

Miracles are usual and expected occurrences in our church. By experience, I can say that man is not just a common creature. He has the fourth dimension in his heart and it is the four dimensional world that takes dominion and control over the material dimensions—the cubical world, the world of the plane and the world of the line.

Through this realm of faith, which is the four dimensional world, you can command your circumstances and situations to change, in the name of Jesus, and give beauty to the ugly and chaotic, while bringing healing to the hurting and suffering people.

3

The Creative Power of Our Spoken Word

There are certain steps we must take in order for faith to be properly incubated, (birthed, developed and to mature), and a central truth we must learn about the realm that faith operates in. There is also a basic principle about the spoken word that we need to understand. So I want to speak about the creative power of the spoken word, and the reason why it is important that we use it.

One morning I was having breakfast with one of Korea's leading neurosurgeons. He told me about the various medical findings on the operation of the brain. He asked, "Dr. Cho, did you know that the speech center in the brain influences all the other nerves? According to our recent findings in Neurology, the speech center in the brain has strong influences over all the other nerves."

Then I laughed and said, "I've known that for a long time."

"How did you know that?" he asked.

I replied that I had learned it from Dr. James.

"Who is this Dr.James?" he asked.

"He was one of the famous doctors in Biblical times nearly two thousand years ago," I replied. "And in his book, chapter three, the first few verses, Dr. James clearly defines the activity and importance of the tongue and the speech center."

The neurosurgeon was completely amazed. "Does the Bible really teach about this?"

"Yes," I answered. "The tongue is the least member of our body, but can bridle the whole body."

Then this neurosurgeon began to expound their findings. He said that the speech nerve center had such power over all of the body that simply speaking can give one control over his body, to manipulate it in the way he wishes. He said, "If someone keeps on saying, 'I'm going to become weak,' then right away all the nerves receive that message and they say, 'Oh, let's prepare for weakness, for we've received instructions from our central communication that we should become weak.' Then, in a natural sequence, they adjust their physical attitudes to weakness."

"If someone says, 'Well, I have no ability. I can't do this job,' then right away all the nerves begin to declare the same thing. 'Right,' they respond, 'we received an instruction from the central nervous system saying that we have no abilities. We should give up striving to develop any capacity for capability. We must prepare ourselves to be part of an incapable person.'

"If someone says, 'I'm very old. I'm so very old, and am tired and can't do anything,' then right away the speech central control responds, giving out orders to that effect. The nerves respond, 'Yes, we are old. We are ready for the grave. Let's be ready to disintegrate.' If someone keeps saying that he is old, then that person is soon going to die."

That neurosurgeon continued saying, "Such a man should never retire. Once he retires, he will keep repeating to himself, 'I am retired,' and all the nerves will start responding and become less active and ready for a quick death."

For a Successful Personal Life

That conversation carried much meaning for me and made a great impact on my life, for I could see that one good usage of the spoken word can create a successful personal life.

People easily adapt themselves to speaking in a negative way. Suppose a man keeps saying, "Boy, am I poor. I don't even have money to give the Lord." When a job offer with good salary comes, his nervous system responds, "I am not able to be rich because I haven't received that reverse instruction from my nerve center yet. I am supposed to be poor, so I can't accept this offer. I can't afford to have the job." Like attracts like, and if you act as if you were a poor person you attract poverty; this attraction, if it remains consistent, will have you permanently dwell in poverty.

Just as James 3:5 said, 2,000 years ago, so it is today. Medical science has just discovered this principle. This neurosurgeon said that people should keep saying to themselves, "I am young. I am able. I still can do the work of a young person no matter what my chronological age is." The nerves of that person will then come alive and thus receive power and strength from the nerve center.

James 3:3 clearly says that whosoever controls the tongue, controls the whole body. What you speak, you are going to get. If you keep on saying that you are poor, then all of your system conditions itself to attract poverty, and you will feel at home in poverty; you would rather be poor. But if you keep on saying that you are able and that you can achieve some success, then all of your body would be motivated to success. You would be ready to meet any challenge and ready to conquer it. This is the reason you should never speak in a negative way but should always speak positively.

Korean people have a habit of making frequent use of words having to do with dying. Common expressions are: "Oh, it's so warm I could die." "Oh, I've eaten so much I could suffocate to death." "Oh, I'm so happy I could die." And "Oh, I'm scared to death." That may be because, throughout Korea's five thousand year history, we have been constantly at war. My generation has never seen total peace in our country. I was born during the World War II, grew up during the Korean War, and I still live on the brink of war even now. Before you can be changed, you must change your language. If you do not change your language, you will not be changed. If you want to see your children changed, you must first teach them to use the proper language. If you want to see rebellious and irresponsible youth changed into responsible adults you must teach them this new language.

Where can we learn this new language? From the best language book of all, the Bible. The Holy Spirit takes the Word, energizes it and makes it become alive to us individually. Read the Bible from Genesis through Revelation. Acquire the Bible's language; speak the word of faith, and feed your life with a vocabulary of constructive, progressive, productive, and victorious words. Speak those words; keep repeating them so that they will have control of your whole body. Then the constructive words you have spoken will condition your whole body, mind and spirit to work toward and to achieve success. This is the first important reason to speak positively: because speaking positively creates the power to have a successful personal life.

For God's Purposes

There is another reason we need to use the creative power of the spoken word. Not only can it help us to be successful in our own lives, but the Holy Spirit also needs us to use it to bring about God's purposes.

When I first entered the ministry I could feel myself in a struggle even while I delivered my sermons, and sensed hindrances in my spirit. Then the Spirit of the Lord would come down into my spirit. In my mind's eyes, as I preached, I could see cancers disappear, tuberculosis healed, cripples leaning heavily on crutches suddenly throw them aside and walk. It was as if I were watching television.

Korea is more than 7,000 miles apart from America, and, back then, I heard very little about this type of deliverance and healing ministry. Even a few missionaries around me were ignorant of this type of ministry. Talking to them about it caused more confusions.

I finally came to the conclusion that this was a hindrance created by Satan. Each time it happened, I would say, "You spirit of hindrance, go in the name of Jesus! I command you to leave me. Get out of me."

But the more I commanded, the more clearly I could see people being healed. I became so desperate I could hardly preach. The visions constantly appeared, so I made it a matter of fasting and praying, waiting upon the Lord.

Then in my heart I heard the Lord say, "Son, that is not a hindrance of Satan. This is a revelational knowledge and the visual desire of the Holy Spirit. It is the Word of Wisdom. God wants to heal these people and He wants you to proclaim God's healing in faith beforehand."

"No," I replied, "I don't understand that. God can do anything without my ever saying a word."

Later, I read, in the first chapter of Genesis, "The earth was without form and void," and the Holy Spirit brooded over the earth but nothing happened. God then revealed an important truth to me. He said, "The presence of the Holy Spirit, the mighty anointing of the Holy Ghost was brooding over the waters. Did anything happen at that point? Did anything change?"

"No," I replied. "Nothing happened."

Then God spoke into my spirit, "You can feel the presence of the Holy Spirit in your church,—the pulsating, permeating presence of the Holy Spirit—but unless you speak the word, nothing might happen. Souls may not be saved or broken homes may not be reunited. You must speak the Word in faith. Then faith building words of life taken by the Holy Spirit and planted into the hearts of the believers will begin to bring results. The Holy Spirit is present, but when you preach, He takes the Word and by His power He creates new life in the hearts of the believers. Don't just beg me and beg me to heal people. The Holy Spirit is present in your services but you must speak the Word in faith. I want to have the material to perform miracles with. When the Holy Spirit was brooding over the earth, I spoke the words, 'Let there be light,' 'Let there be firmament,' and they came into being. I have placed words of faith in your mouth and sent the Holy Spirit into the service, too. Speak these words out, 'Be healed in Jesus' Name!' 'Cancer, go, in Jesus' Name' and the Word and the Holy Spirit will work together."

The realization of that truth was a turning point in my life. I apologized to God: "Father, I'm sorry. I'll speak forth."

But when I stood before the people I was still afraid for no one had taught me anything along these lines and I wanted to be sure. I was afraid that nothing might happen when I spoke. I wondered what people would say. Surely it would be new to them. So I said to God, "Since I'm afraid, I'm not going to speak out about the crippled people that I see healed, or the cancer disappearing. Father, I'll start with headaches."

After this, while I was preaching, visions of various healing continued to spring up in my spirit; but I continued to ignore them. I would only speak out, "Someone here is being healed of a headache," and instantly that person would be healed. I was amazed that just by speaking out the healing I saw, people were actually healed of headaches. I pondered these things in my heart and marveled at the truth the Holy Spirit was teaching me. I just wanted to be sure these new thoughts and insights were from God.

Little by little I gained courage. I began to speak that sinuses were healed, then deaf people were healed, and finally I began to speak out about all the healing the Holy Spirit witnessed in my spirit that were taking place. Now, in our church on Sunday mornings hundreds of people receive healing this way. Because of multiple services on Sundays and the limitation of time in each service, I must act quickly. So while I am still standing after prayer, the Lord shows me the healing that are taking place and I call them out. I simply close my eyes and speak forth. In recognition of the fact that they have been healed, people stand up. They stand when the particular disease or illness they have is called out. During this part of a service, many people from all over the auditorium rise to claim their healing.

I learned one truth from this. The Holy Spirit prepares people's hearts through anointed preaching. And the Spirit wants to heal diseases and perform miracles with proper material—our spoken word of faith. When we speak out the word of faith, we will see miracles happen. If the Holy Spirit imparts faith into your heart to remove a mountain, do not pray and beg for the mountain to be moved; rather, speak: "Be removed to yonder sea!" and it shall come to pass. If you learn this, and make it a habit to speak under the anointing of the Holy Spirit, with the faith that God has given you, you will see many miracles in your life. When the Holy Spirit sees your faith, He will choose to work in your behalf.

Ministering to 700,000 regular attending members is not an easy task. We have a 24-hour telephone ministry service in our church with counselors staying around the clock by shifts, to receive calls and pray for those in need. I try to keep my home phone number unregistered, but my home number soon becomes known somehow and I receive calls practically all day long.

Many nights, at 10:00 p.m., when I'm already in bed, a call comes with a plea, "Pastor, my grandson has a high fever, please pray for him." So I pray.

Eleven o'clock another call comes, "My husband is not yet home from his business. Please pray." And I pray.

Then at twelve o'clock midnight, the phone rings and a crying wife says, "My husband came home and beat me up. It's so terrible that I don't want to live." So I counsel with her.

At one o'clock I receive a call from a drunken man saying, "My wife attends your church; why do you teach her to behave in such a way?" Then I will give him a full explanation.

In mid-morning a telephone call comes from a hospital, "Pastor, such and such a person is dying now in this hospital. His last desire before dying is to see you. Would you come quickly?" So I make a plan to rush to the hospital.

One night, the telephone rang so much during the night that I unplugged the cord so that I could get some sleep.

But the Holy Spirit spoke to my heart, "Is that being a good shepherd? A good shepherd would never leave his sheep stranded." So, I got up and put the cord back into the wall. One advantage I have when traveling abroad is that I finally get a good night's sleep.

In a very cold winter night, I went to bed and pulled the covers up. I was appreciating the cozy warmth of my bed, and had almost fallen asleep when a telephone call came: "Pastor, do you know who this is?"

"Of course I do. I married you and your wife!"

"I have tried for two years with all there is within me to make our marriage work but it is not working," he said. "Tonight we had a big argument and we finally decided to separate. We have already divided our assets. But there's just one thing,—we want a blessing from you. We were married with your blessing and we want to be divorced with your blessing."

What a position for a minister to be in, to bless them in marriage and now to bless them in divorce! I replied, "Can you wait until tomorrow? It's too cold, and I'm settled in bed. Must I come now?"

"Pastor," he said disappointedly, "Tomorrow will be too late. We're leaving each other today. We don't want you to preach to us. It's too late for that. We're beyond reach now; just come and simply give us your blessing so that we can be divorced."

I crawled out of bed and went into the living room. In my heart, I was angry at Satan. "This is the work of the devil," I thought. "It is not the work of the Holy Spirit."

As I began to pray, my spirit rose to the the spiritual realm, to the higher dimensional world. I knelt down in the quietness of the night and closed my eyes. I saw the cross of Jesus where every need was met through His shed blood. By the help of the Holy Spirit I began to see this family restored and their marriage renewed. I saw a clear picture of this and prayed, "Oh, Father, make it happen just like that."

While I was praying, I was touched by the faith of God and in the name of Jesus Christ this entire situation was changed in the spiritual realm. I saw it and I believed it as I prayed, then I went to visit the couple.

They were living in a very luxurious apartment with all the convenient stuff one could wish for. But when I walked in, I felt an icy chill. I felt the hatred that existed between that couple. You know, you can have all the material goods of this world, but if there is hatred in your family, the wealth of material goods means absolutely nothing at all. They are not a blessing.

I came in and I found the husband sitting in the living room. His wife was in the bedroom. As soon as I walked into the living room the husband began to speak in a derogatory manner about his wife. His wife then rushed out of the bedroom and said, "Don't listen to him! Listen to me." Then she began to speak out against him.

As I listened to the man, everything he said seemed to be right. Then, as I listened to the woman, everything she said seemed to be right. Each was perfectly right in his or her own eyes. Both were right and I was sandwiched in between.

Both said they were completely finished in their marriage. "Don't pray for us," they kept repeating. "Just pray for our divorce."

But in my prayer, I had already overruled the three dimensional world by seeing in the higher dimension and praying in faith that this marriage was healed. Being confident that I had heard from the Holy Spirit about them, I took the hand of the husband and the hand of the wife and I said, "In the name of Jesus Christ, I command Satan to loose his hold of hatred on this couple. And at this moment, in the mighty name of Jesus Christ, I command that these two be melted together again. Let their hearts be melted and rejoined in love and harmony instead of going through with a divorce."

Suddenly, I felt a warm drop fall on my hand. When I looked at the man, he was crying and I saw his tears had fallen on my hand.

I thought, "Praise God! It is working!"

When I looked at the eyes of his wife, I could see that her eyes were watering also. I drew their hands together and said, "What the Lord has joined together, let no man or circumstances divide."

I stood up and said, "I'm going."

Both of them followed me out to the gate, and as I left they both said, "Goodbye, Pastor."

"Praise God," I said. "It works!" When you know that the Bible teaches against divorce and you see a couple in the spiritual realm as restored, this is seeing in the higher dimension.

The next Sunday, both of them were in the choir and sang beautifully. After the service, I shook their hands and asked the wife, "What happened?"

"Well, we don't know," she answered. "But when you said those words and gave such strong commands, we felt something break down in our hearts. It was as if a wall had been destroyed, and we were shaken.

"When the wall was destroyed, we began to feel that perhaps we should try once more, together. After you left, we spent the night unpacking all of our things. Now, when we think of it, we cannot understand why we argued so much and why we were going to separate. Now, we love each other more than ever."

The Holy Spirit wants you to speak the word! He wants me to speak the word! If I had pled with them or silently prayed for them, I would have missed the target. As far as the Holy Spirit was concerned the marriage was healed as I saw it in the higher dimension. I simply took authority over the spirit of hatred and commanded it to be broken in the name of Jesus. The spoken word of faith brings results.

Jesus used the spoken word to change and create. Jesus' disciples also used the spoken word to change and create. Unfortunately, the Church of Jesus Christ seems to have become a perennial beggar, begging and begging, afraid to speak forth commanding words filled with faith. We need to learn to speak forth words of command as Jesus did.

Entering the Presence of Jesus Christ

There is power in the spoken word to bring you into the presence of Jesus. When you read Romans 10:10, you will find, "With the heart man believeth unto righteousness; and with the mouth confession is made unto salvation." It is through confession of faith that man can grasp and understand salvation that comes by only Jesus Christ.

Nowhere in the scripture does it indicate that someone must go up to heaven and bring Jesus Christ down to earth to give salvation. What the scripture says is that the words that can result in salvation are near, for they are the words in your heart and in your mouth, prompted by the Holy Spirit.

Where is Jesus Christ in this process? What is his address? He is not high up in the sky nor below the ground. Jesus is in His Word revealed to us by the power of the Holy Spirit.

Where are the words that can result in your salvation? They are in your heart and in your mouth! He regards the sincerity of your heart and so he answers to you when you speak in faith. Just as you can enter the presence of Jesus through your spoken word, you can release the power of Jesus through your definite spoken word of faith. If you do not speak the word of faith clearly, Jesus Christ may not manifest Himself. The Bible says, "Whatsoever you bind on earth shall be bound in heaven, and whatsoever you release on earth shall be released in heaven." (Matt. 16:19) In Greek, this verse is written in the past perfect tense stating that it has already been released. You can speak the command of this promise and release men and women from bondage or release the word of faith and the presence of Jesus will confirm the word spoken.

When I meet with my 750 associate pastors, I tell them that it is their responsibility to live in the presence of Jesus Christ and to take His presence with them wherever they go. "To be in Jesus and meet specific needs is what you must do," is my command. Let me give you some examples.

In our vicinity, there are several churches of different denominations. In one particular Presbyterian Church, the minister speaks only about the born again experience. He speaks strongly only about the salvation experience so his messages draw men and women to Christ and they receive salvation, but no more than that.

The Holiness Church nearby preaches about sanctification. "Be sanctified. Be sanctified," they exhort repeatedly. Many people attend that church and receive a touch of sanctification. The pastor's preaching about the sanctifying Christ is accomplishing sanctification in the lives of his people.

But in our church, I believe it is necessary to preach the full gospel, the total work of Jesus Christ and the Holy Spirit in the life of a believer. The message from our church is about the saving Jesus, the sanctifying Christ, the baptizing Savior, the "blessing" Son of God, the healing Jesus and our soon coming King! The total message for the total man and his total needs creates the presence of the all-sufficient Christ for every need of people today.

Your Role

You enter into the presence of Jesus through the words of your faith. If you speak of salvation, the work of the Holy Spirit will prepare the hearts of people to receive salvation. If you speak about divine healing, faith will rise in the hearts of sick people causing them to reach out for healing in that service. If you preach about the miracle-performing Christ, the presence of the miracle-performing Christ will come into that service and confirm the confession of your mouth. He uses your words of faith. If the word is not spoken clearly because of fear, the longing for these manifestations will be present but the manifestation of His power to those in need may not appear. So speak the word clearly and speak it out boldly!

Many people have various problems in their homes today because they do not have family altars. If the father maintains a family altar and speaks clearly and distinctly about the presence of Jesus Christ in his home to the family, the presence of Jesus will be felt in their home and He will take care of their family problems. But since many neglect the family altar, Christian faith is not taught clearly at homes so the children are left without the blessing of knowing the presence of the Holy Spirit to guide their lives.

Regarding gifts, you do not need to wait until you receive any special spiritual gift to lead your family. I have always said that spiritual gifts reside in the Holy Spirit. You, yourself, can never own a spiritual gift but the Holy Spirit will manifest a gift through you when a gift is needed and you are in tune with Him.

Suppose I had the gift of healing. Then indiscriminately I would heal everyone who sought me for healing. If I had the gift, I would give it to everyone; I would not be truly discerning. The Holy Spirit, however, sees a need and then allows the operation of a gift to flow through someone to meet that need.

It is important to remember that all the gifts reside in the Holy Spirit and it is the Holy Spirit who dwells in your church and in you. Through Him, you could have any kind of ministry,—the ministry of teaching, the ministry of evangelism, the ministry of missions, the ministry of pastoring and the ministry of divine healing. The Holy Spirit will use you and manifest Himself through you as

His channel. So do not worry about your acquisition of any of the gifts.

But be bold! Receive the gift of boldness, then speak the word. Speak the word clearly and the presence of Jesus Christ will draw near and manifest Himself in your services. Bring your congregation into the presence of the Lord and you will see definite and specific results. A father can lead his family into the presence of the Lord through speaking the word boldly, and the Holy Spirit will take care of all of his family's needs. In the same way, I come to my pulpit to preach and plant specific seeds of truth to harvest specific results.

I often see a great fault in many church services. Pastors preach tremendously wonderful messages to their people but right after the preaching, the services are dismissed and the people are sent home. They have not been given time to pray, to allow the Word to take root in their hearts and to bear fruit.

Many churches dismiss their services too soon. Give your congregation time! Shorten the preliminaries and entertainment. Give them the Word and then let them have more time to pray together. Let the Word of God have time to be digested. If more pastors did this, they would see consistent Christian growth and development among their people resulting in church growth.

Ultimately your words mold your life for your speech center influences all of your nerves to respond to the words you speak. When a person receives a full manifestation of the infilling of the Holy Spirit, the Holy Spirit takes over this speech center and, consequently, all the nerves of the body too. When he takes full control, He also enables the believer to control his life.

Speak the word to control and to bridle your whole body and life. When you speak the Word, the Holy Spirit will enable you to control your life and to fulfill what you have spoken.

Preach the Word. Then it goes forth in the power of the Holy Spirit and miracles will be performed in your church confirming the Word you have preached.

Does God use men and women only because they are completely sanctified? No. As long as a Christian lives, he will be struggling with the flesh. God uses you because you have faith and have exercised the Word in faith. So let us make use of the power of our spoken word more and more, to be successful in our personal life, to be used by the Holy Spirit for His desires, and to live in the presence of the Lord everyday.

Remember that Christ manifests Himself through you as you speak forth the Word. What are you going to do with this Jesus Who is using your tongue? Are you going to let Him use you to bless the hurting world and others who have needs? Or will you disobey Him by remaining silent with your mouth shut? The choice is yours. May God bless you as you make your decision.

4

The Spoken Word of God

Our spoken word has creative power and its proper usage is vital to a victorious Christian life. This spoken word, however, must have a correct basis to be truly effective. The principle for discovering the correct basis for the spoken word is one of the most important portions of God's truth. It is this topic that I want to share with you now.

Faith in God's Word

One day, a lady was carried into my office on a stretcher. She was paralyzed from her neck down, and could not even move her fingers. As she was being carried into my office on a stretcher, I began to sense a strange feeling. It felt as if my heart was being troubled. Just as there was an expectation at the pool of Bethesda, I knew that something was going to happen to this lady.

I walked to her stretcher and when I looked into her eyes I realized that she already had the faith to be healed; not a dead faith but a living faith. I touched her forehead with my hand and said, "Sister, in the name of Jesus be healed."

Instantly, the power of God came upon her and she was healed. She stood up from her stretcher, thrilled, frightened and amazed.

She later came to my home with gifts and after entering my study, she asked, "Could I please close the door?"

"Yes," I replied. "Close the door." Then she knelt down before me, still amazed that she had been healed, and said, "Sir, please reveal yourself to me.

"Are you the second incarnate Jesus?"

I laughed. "Dear sister, you know that I eat three meals a day, go to the bathroom, and sleep at night. I am as human as you are, and the only way I have salvation is through Jesus Christ."

This woman had received such a miraculous healing

that the word of it instantly spread. Soon afterward one rich woman came to the church, also being carried in on a stretcher. She had been a Christian for a long time, and a deaconess in her church. She had memorized scripture after scripture regarding divine healing: "I am the Lord that healeth thee." (Ex. 15:26); "With His stripes we are healed." (Isa. 53:5); "He Himself took our infirmities, and bore our sickness." (Matt. 8:17); "And these signs shall follow them that believe...they shall lay hands on the sick, and they shall recover." (Mark 16:17,18)

So I prayed for her with all my might, but nothing happened. Then I shouted, repeating the same prayers for healing. I used the Word of God, and I even jumped, but nothing happened. I asked her to stand up by faith. Many times she tried to stand, but the moment I took my hand away, she fell down like a piece of dead wood. Then I would say, "Have more faith and stand up." Again she tried to stand up, and again she fell down. She would claim that she had all the faith in the world, yet her faith never worked.

I became quite depressed and eventually she began to cry. She claimed, "Pastor, you are prejudiced. You loved that woman so much that you healed her. But you don't really love me. So I am still sick. You are prejudiced."

"Sister," I replied, "I have done everything. You saw me. I have prayed. I have cried. I have jumped and shouted. I did everything that any Pentecostal preacher can do, but nothing happened, and I can't understand why you are not healed."

In my church this bothersome problem of one being healed while another remaining ill has not limited itself to this one occasion. World famous evangelists have come to my church and enthusiastically preached, "Everyone is going to be healed! Everyone of you!" They poured out words of faith, and many people would receive healing.

But then when they would leave, witnessing all the glory, I would be left to contend with those who had not been healed. These people would come to me, discouraged and cast down, and say, "We are not healed. God has given up on us. We are completely forgotten. Why should we continue to struggle to come to Jesus Christ and believe?"

Then I cried and travailed in prayer, "Why Father? Why should it be like this? God, please give me the answer, a very clear-cut answer." And He did. So now I would like to share with you this answer and some realizations that led me to this understanding.

People think that they can believe on the Word of God. They can. But they fail to differentiate between the Word of God which gives general knowledge about God and the Word of God which God uses to impart faith about specific circumstances into a man's heart. It is this latter type of faith which brings miracles.

There are two Greek words for "Word", having slightly different nuances. The universe was created by the Word of God. The Word, stretching from Genesis through Revelation, directly and indirectly, speaks about Jesus Christ, Who is the Word Himself. By reading the Word of God from Genesis to Revelation, you can receive all the knowledge you need about God and His promises. But you do not receive faith just by reading it. You have received knowledge and understanding about God but you have not necessarily received faith for something specific from God.

Romans 10:17 shows us that the material used to build faith is more than just reading God's Word: "Faith cometh by hearing, and hearing by the Word of God." In this scripture, the "Word" has a more specific aspect. Faith specifically comes by hearing the Word of God.

Here is my definition of the Word of God in the practical realm. There are two aspects of the Word of God: one is the written Word of God and the other is the spoken Word of God to a specific person in a specific situation.

Many years ago, a Korean lady Ms. Yum Hae-Kyung, had a very big youth meeting on Samgak Mountain. She had a great ministry to Korean youngsters. When she stood up, people would come forward and fell down, seized by the power of the Holy Spirit. Many young people would flock to her meetings and when she held a youth campaign on Samgak Mountain, thousands of young people went to it.

During the week of one youth campaign it rained heavily and all the rivers overflowed. A group of young people wanted to go to the town on the opposite side of the river where the meetings were being held. But when they came to the crossing, they found out that the banks of the river had overflowed there, too. They could not find a bridge or a boat, and thus most of them became discouraged.

But three girls got together and said, "Why can't we just wade through the waters? Peter walked on the water and Peter's God is our God; his Jesus is our Jesus and his faith is our faith. Peter believed and we should believe even more. We are going to walk on this river."

The banks of the river had overflowed but these three girls knelt down, held hands together, quoting the scriptures concerning the story of Peter walking on the water and claimed they could believe in the same way. Then, in the sight of their group, they shouted and began to wade through the water.

Immediately they were swept away by the raging torrent and three days later their dead bodies were found in the open sea.

This incident caused repercussions throughout Korea. Non Christian newspapers carried the story, making headlines of it: "Their God Could Not Save Them," "Why Did God Not Answer Their Prayer of Faith?" So unbelievers had a real heyday as a result of this occurrence and the Christian church experienced a slump, feeling depressed and discouraged because they had no adequate answer.

This became a target of severe blames all over Korea and many previously good Christians lost their faith. They would say, "These girls believed exactly as our ministers have taught; they exercised their faith. From the platform our pastors constantly urges the people to boldly exercise their faith in the Word of God. These girls did that, so why didn't God answer? Jehovah God can-not be a living God. This must be only a formalistic religion we have been involved in."

What kind of answer would you have given to these people? Those girls had believed. They had exercised their faith based on the Word of God.

But God had no reason to support their faith. Peter never walked on the water because of what is written in the Bible, which gives general knowledge about God. Peter required that Christ give a specific word to him. Peter asked, "Lord, if you are Jesus, command me to come." Jesus replied, "Come!"

The word that Christ gave to Peter was the spoken Word of God. He gave a specific word, "Come," to a specific person, Peter, in a specific situation, a storm.

The spoken Word of God brings faith. Faith comes by hearing and hearing, from the Word of God. Peter never walked on the water by knowledge of God alone. Peter had received the spoken Word from Jesus.

But these girls only had the written Word and their human-centered faith. They exercised their human faith on the written Word. That was their fundamental mistake. They should have prayed to God before they went into the river. I know that they never had received spoken Word of God at that time. God, therefore, had no respon-sibility to support their faith and the difference between the way these girls exercised their faith and the way Peter exercised his faith is as great as the difference between night and day.

The written Word of God usually gives you "head faith" which means rather knowledge of God than the wonder working faith. But when the Holy Spirit comes on you and pour out His answer on the Word, it brings "belly faith" which gives you boldness and firm assurance of the Word of God. When we have such "belly faith," we can have miracles.

Several years ago, two Bible school graduates failed completely in their first venture into the ministry. These two young men were my disciples. They listened to my sermons, came to my church and learned the concept of the principles of faith.

They began their first venture into ministry with what seemed to be a great deal of faith, clinging to such scriptures as: "Open your mouth wide and I will fill it." (Psalm 81:10); "If ye ask anything in my name, I will do it." (John 14:14)

They went to a bank and drew a large sum loan. Then they went to a rich man and made another large sum personal loan. With this money they bought land and built a beautiful sanctuary without even having any congregation. They began preaching, expecting the people to flock in by the hundreds and their debts to be paid. But nothing like that happened.

One of these ministers had borrowed approximately $30,000 and the other one about $50,000. Soon their creditors came to collect their payments and these young men were cornered in a terrible situation, arriving at a point where they almost lost their faith in God.

Then they both came to me. They cried, "Pastor Cho, why is your God different from our God? You had started with $2,500 and you completed a five million dollar project. We went out and built things which cost total of $80,000 only. Why wouldn't God answer us? We believed in the same God and we exercised the same faith. So why hasn't He answered?"

Then they started quoting the scriptures containing promises from the Old and New Testaments adding, "We did exactly as you taught us but we failed."

Then I replied, "I am glad that you have failed after hearing my word. Surely you are my disciples, but you have not been the disciples of Jesus Christ. You have misunderstood my teaching. I started my church with the spoken Word of God. God clearly spoke to my heart, saying, "Rise up! Go out and build a church which will seat 10,000 people." God imparted His faith to my heart and I went out and obeyed and a miracle occurred. But you went out with a general knowledge about God. God therefore had no responsibility to support you, even though your ministry was for the Lord Jesus Christ."

Brothers and sisters, you come to know God through the written Word of God. You gain understanding and knowledge about Him. But the written Word of God does not always become the spoken Word of God for you.

Suppose a sick man would have gone to the pool of Bethesda and said to those around it, "You foolish fellows, why are you waiting here? This is always the same pool in the same location with the same water. Why should you wait here day after day? I'm just going to jump in and wash myself."

Then he might have dived in and washed himself. But if he were to come out of the water, he would not have been healed. It was only after the angel of the Lord came and troubled the water that the people could jump in, wash and be healed. Yet it was still the same pool of Bethesda, at the same location, with the same water. Only when the water was troubled by God's angel could a miracle occur.

The spoken Word of God is produced out of the written Word. The written Word of God is like the pool of Bethesda. You may listen to the Word of God and you may study the Bible, but only when the Holy Spirit comes and quickens a scripture or scriptures to your specific situation, does the written Word of God become the spoken Word of God.

The written Word of God is given to everybody. The written Word is common to Koreans, Europeans, Africans and Americans. It is given to all so that all many gain knowledge about God. But the spoken Word of God is not given to everyone at all times. It is given to a specific person who is waiting upon the Lord until the Holy Spirit quickens the written Word into the spoken Word of God. If you never have time to wait upon the Lord, then the Lord can never come and quicken the needed scripture to your heart.

This is a busy age. People come to church and are entertained; they hear a short sermon and are dismissed, without having any time of waiting upon the Lord. They get the written Word, but since they do not receive the spoken Word of God, they miss out on seeing the miraculous workings of God, and begin to doubt His power.

We must come to the sanctuary, listen attentively to the preaching and wait upon the Lord. But people do not come and listen prayerfully to the message, waiting upon the Lord to receive the spoken Word of God: therefore, they cannot receive the faith they need for the solutions to their problems. Their knowledge of the Bible may increase as they come to church. But their problems are still there and nothing happens to change them. So they begin to fall away and lose faith.

Another problem with many churches in this active age is that ministers are busy with too many matters. They spend hours and hours as janitors, financiers, contractors, doing construction work and going in hundred different directions.

By Saturday they are so tired that they fumble around to find some Word to preach on. They are so tired that they have no time to wait upon the Lord, no time to change the green grass into white milk. Their congregations are simply fed grass and not given the milk of the Word. This is a serious mistake.

Lay persons are not the pastor's enemies but his friends. As the apostles did, so should the minister concentrate on prayer and the ministering of the Word of

God, delegating any other type of work to his deacons, deaconesses and other lay leaders.

I follow this pattern in my church, and I dare not go up to the platform without first waiting upon the Lord and receiving the spoken Word of God that God would have me give for that service. If I do not receive the spoken Word of God, I will not go to the platform.

So, I go to our prayer mountain on Saturday, crawl into a prayer grotto, close the door and sit there until the Holy Spirit comes and gives me God's spoken Word. Sometimes I stay the whole night through during that time praying, "Lord, tomorrow the people are coming with all kinds of problems,—sickness, disease, family problems, problems in business—every type of problem that can be imagined.

"They are coming not only to hear general knowledge about You, but they are also coming to receive real solutions to their problems. If we don't give them a living faith, then they are going to go back home without receiving their solutions. I need to have a specific message for the specific people on this specific Sunday."

Then I wait until God gives me that message. When coming to the platform, I march in like a general, knowing that the message I preach is under the anointing of the Holy Spirit.

After I preach, people in the congregation come to me and say, "Pastor, your sermon was exactly what I needed. I've got the faith that my problem will be solved." This is because I helped supply to them God's spoken Word.

Brothers and sisters, we are not building a holy country club in the church. We rather deal with matters of life and death. If the pastor does not supply the spoken Word of God to his people, then you have only a religious club. In the social world one can already see organizations such as the Kiwanis Clubs and Rotary Clubs, and their members pay a type of tithes, too.

The churches we build should be places where people get their solutions from the Lord, receive miracles for their lives and can gain not just a knowledge about God but get to know Him in a vital way. To carry out such purposes, the pastors must first receive the spoken Word of God.

Christians should be given time to wait upon the Lord so that the Holy Spirit can have a full opportunity to deal with their lives and inspire them through the scripture. The Holy Spirit can take scripture, the "said Word" of God and apply it to a person's heart, making it the "saying Word" of God.

Now I can tell you why so many people cannot receive healing. All the promises are potentially, but not literally, yours. Never simply pick a promise out of God's Word and say, "Oh, this is mine; I will repeat it over and over again. This is mine. This is mine!" No! It is potentially yours, yes, but make it yours in a practical reality by waiting upon the Lord.

Before the Lord quickens a scripture to an individual, the Lord has many things to do. The Lord wants to cleanse your life and make you surrender to Him. The

Lord will never give promises promiscuously. As the Lord deals with you, take time to wait upon Him, confessing your sins and surrendering your life to Him. When these conditions are met, then the power of God will come. Your heart, like the pool of Bethesda, will be troubled by a particular scripture and you will know that its promise is yours, and you will have the faith to bring about the needed miracle.

God's Uppermost Goal

The healing of the physical body is not the Spirit's ultimate goal. You must know where the priority lies. His ultimate goal is the healing of your soul. When God deals with you, He will always deal with you through the healing of your soul. If your soul is not right with God, no amount of praying, shouting or jumping will bring the spoken Word of God for healing to you.

You must first get right with the Lord. Confess your sins, apply the blood of Jesus Christ, be saved and receive eternal life, then the Holy Spirit will prick your heart with a scripture of divine healing, inspire you, and give you the spoken Word that you need. But in order for this to happen, you must wait on the Lord.

Divine healing is completely according to God's sovereign will. Sometimes a person receives an instant healing from his disease. Another person may have to wait a longer time and sometimes a person may not be healed at all.

One of our church's finest deacons became ill. This deacon had given everything to the Lord. He loved God and worked for the Lord in an amazing way. He was told that he had a cancer growth inside of his body and the doctor wanted to operate on him. But our church members knew that God was going to heal him, for he was such a wonderful saint with great faith. This was their reasoning.

I prayed for his healing. All of our 40,000 members at that time prayed, storming the throne of grace. And that deacon claimed the healing.

But nothing happened. He became even worse instead. Eventually he bled so badly that he was carried to the hospital and operated on. Many of my members were worried and complained, "Where is God? Why is God treating him like this?"

But I praised God, for I knew that He had some specific purpose in what was happening.

When he was hospitalized in the ward, he began to preach the gospel to all the people with whom he made contact. Soon every person on every floor in that hospital knew that there was a living Jesus, because His representative was right in their hospital. Many doctors, nurses and patients at that time became saved.

Then our members rejoiced, saying, "Praise God. It was far better for him to be in the hospital than to be divinely healed immediately at home."

God showed that His first priority was the eternal healing of souls rather than the earthly healing of the physical.

When there is pain and suffering, we are apt to cry out for immediate deliverance. But this we should not do. If your suffering should bring about redemptive grace or if your suffering becomes the channel for the flowing of God's redeeming grace to others, then your suffering has been God-appointed. If, however, your suffering causes you to become an invalid and starts to destroy you, then this is from Satan and you should pray through and rid yourself of it.

I will relay to you one case in which God did not deliver people from their suffering.

It was during the Korean War when 500 ministers were captured and killed and two thousand churches were destroyed. The communists were vicious to the ministers. One minister's family was captured in the city of Inchon, Korea. The communist leaders put them on what they called a "People's Trial." The accusers would say, "One man is guilty of causing this kind of sin, and for that kind of sin it is proper that he be punished."

The only response then given would be a chorus of voices agreeing, "Yah, Yah!"

This time they dug a large hole, putting the pastor, his wife, and several of his children in. The leader then spoke, "Mister, all these years you misled the people with

the superstition of the Bible. Now if you publicly renounce the Bible before these people, and repent of this
misdemeanor, then you, your wife, and your children will
be freed. But if you insist in believing your superstitions,
all of you will be buried alive. Make a decision!"

All of his children then cried out, "Oh Daddy! Daddy!
Think of us, Daddy!"

Think of it! If you had been in his place, what would
you have done? I am the father of three children and
would almost feel like going to hell rather than see my
children killed.

This father was shaken. He lifted up his hand and
said, "Yes, yes, I'll do it. I am going to renounce my..."

But before he could finish his sentence his wife
nudged him saying, "Darling, say NO!"

"Hush, children," she said. "Tonight we are going to
have supper with the King of kings, the Lord of lords!"

She led them in singing, "In the Sweet Bye and Bye."
The whole family were to be buried alive. They kept
singing until the soil came up to their necks, while all the
people watching it. God did not deliver them, but almost
all the people who watched this execution became
Christians, many of who are now members of my church.

Through their suffering, the grace of redemption
flowed. God gave His only begotten Son to be crucified
on the cross so that this world could be saved and
redeemed. That is God's uppermost goal—the redemption of souls. So when you desire divine healing, or an

answer from above, always focus your desire through the lenses of God's uppermost goal, the redeeming of souls. If you see that your suffering brings about more redemption than your healing, then do not ask for deliverance, but ask God to give you strength to persevere.

It is not always easy to discern between the suffering brought by Satan that God would rather deliver, and the suffering that God would use to bring about the flow of redemptive grace. To discern good and evil, you need to wait upon the Lord and to know the will of the Lord. Do not become discouraged or go from one famous evangelist to another to receive their words. But let God show you His will through your prayer, fasting and faith.

When the Holy Spirit quickens the written Word to you, a miraculous faith will be imparted to your heart. You will know that the scripture no longer belongs to the "said Word" of God, but is instantly the "saying Word" of God for you. You must then stand upon that Word and go ahead and do it, even though your whole life seems as dark as midnight. Once you receive the spoken Word of God, do not be frightened. Just go ahead and walk on the water and you will see a miracle. Be careful, however, not to move ahead of God.

Many people do move ahead of God, even as Paul did in his eagerness to bring the gospel of Jesus Christ. Jesus commanded His disciples to go to the ends of the world and preach the gospel so Paul went out on the Word of God and headed for Asia. But the Holy Spirit did not permit him to go there.

Then Paul said, "I will go to Bithynia." But again the Holy Spirit said, "NO!"

Paul and his company then went down to Troas, an unknown city. We can imagine his wondering there. He was confused, thinking to himself, "I was just obeying the command of Jesus. Jesus said we should go into all the world and preach the gospel. Why am I a failure?"

But as he was praying and waiting upon the Lord, he received the spoken Word of God. A man from Macedonia appeared in a vision and said, "Come over into Macedonia and help us!" So he took a boat and crossed over to Europe.

In Paul's example we can again see the difference between the written Word and the spoken Word of God.

Receiving the Spoken Word of God

People have come to me and commented, "Pastor Cho, I can pray through about the various promises from the scriptures, and I can wait until the Holy Spirit quickens and applies them to me. But how can I get the spoken Word of God about choosing a husband or a wife? I read all the scriptures, but the Bible does not say whether I should go marry Elizabeth, Mary or Joan. How can I get the spoken Word of God about this?

"Also, the Bible does not say that you should go and live in Lakeland, Los Angeles, or some northern area.

How can I receive God's will about that?"

These are legitimate questions. Let me show you the five steps I use to understand God's will or to receive the spoken Word of God about these decisions.

Neutral Gear

My first step is to put myself in "neutral gear," not forward or backward but completely calm in my heart. Then I wait upon the Lord: "Lord, I'm here waiting before You, hoping to hear You speak into my spirit. If You say 'yes,' I will go; if you say 'no,' I will not go. I don't wish to make any decisions for my own benefit. I want to decide according to Your desire for me. Whether it is good or bad for me, I only want Your guidance." With this attitude I wait upon the Lord. Many times the best action to take is to fast and pray, for if you eat too much you will become so tired that you will not be able to pray. Then, if you know you are really calmed down, you can come to the second step.

Divine Desire

The second thing I do is to ask the Lord to reveal His will through my desire. God always comes to you through your sanctified desire. "Delight thyself also in the

Lord; and He shall give thee the desires of thine heart." (Psalm 37:4)   "The desire of the righteous shall be granted." (Proverbs 10:24)   "What things soever ye desire, when ye pray, believe that ye receive them, and ye shall have them." (Mark 11:24)

Desire, then, is one of God's focusing points.   Moreover, Philippians 2:13 reads, "For it is God which worketh in you both to will and to do of his good pleasure."

Through the Holy Spirit, God puts His desire in your heart and the will to do His will.   So pray to the Lord, "Lord, now give me the divine desire according to Your own will."

Wait on the Lord and pray until you pray through: until God gives you His divine desire.   As you pray, many desires, beautiful desires, will probably flow into your heart.   In your praying then, also have the patience to wait for God's desire to settle in.   Do not stand up and say, "Oh, I've got everything," and rush away.   Wait upon the Lord a little longer.   Desires can come from Satan, from your own spirit or from the Holy Spirit.   As you wait before the Lord with an open heart to know His will, one desire will rise above the others accompanied by great peace.

Time is always the test.   If you wait patiently, your own desire or the desires from Satan will become greatly weakened, but the desires from the Holy Spirit will become stronger and stronger.   So, wait and receive the divine desire.

Scriptural Screening

When the right desire from the Holy Spirit has come into clear and sharp focus, then I proceed to step three: I compare the desire I have with what the Bible has to say to confirm it.

One day a lady came to me. All excited, she said, "Oh Pastor Cho, I am going to support your ministry with a large sum of money."

"Praise God," I exclaimed. "Have a seat and tell me about this."

She exclaimed, "I have a fantastic desire to go into business. This business deal is going on, and if I join in I think I can make big money."

"What kind of business is it?" I asked.

She said, "I have a burning desire to get a monopoly on the cigarette business. Tobacco, you know."

"Forget about it," I retorted.

"But I have the desire!" she exclaimed, "the burning desire, just like you preached about."

"That desire is from your own flesh," I replied. "Have you ever gone through the Bible to see if what you would be doing is scriptural?"

"No!"

"Your desire must be screened through the scripture," I instructed her. The Bible says that you are the temple of the Holy Spirit (I Cor. 3:16; 6:19). If God ever wanted His people to smoke, then He would have made our noses differently. Smoke stacks are supposed to be open upward to the sky not downward. Think about our nose; it is not pointing upward to the sky but downward. God did not purpose that people should smoke, because our smoke stacks are upside down. Your body is the Holy Spirit's dwelling place. If you pollute it with smoke, then you are polluting the temple of the Holy Spirit with smoke. Your desire is out of the will of God. It would be best if you just forget about this new business."

One man came to me and said, "Pastor, I've struck up a friendship with a beautiful and wonderful woman, a widow. She is sweet, beautiful and wonderful and when I pray, I have a burning desire to marry her. But I also have my own wife and children."

"Look," I replied, "You forget about this because it is from the devil."

"Oh, no, no. This is not from the devil," he disagreed. "When I prayed, the Holy Spirit spoke in my heart and told me that my wife was not exactly the right kind of rib to fit into my side. My present wife is always a thorn in my flesh. The Holy Spirit spoke and said that this widow is my lost rib, which will fit exactly into my side."

I said to him, "That is not from the Holy Spirit. That's from the devil's spirit because it's already against the scripture."

Many people make this kind of mistake. If they pray against the written Word of God, then the devil will speak.

The Holy Spirit will never contradict God's written Word. That man did not listen to me, but he divorced his wife and married that widow. He is now of all men the most miserable. He found out that his second rib was even worse than his first.

So all of our desires should be carefully screened with the scripture. If you do not have the self-confidence to do this yourself, then go to your minister or pastor.

A Beckoning Signal

After I screen my desire through the written Word, the teachings of God, then I am ready for step four: to ask God for a beckoning signal from my circumstances. If God has truly spoken to your heart, He will certainly give you a signal from the external world.

When Elijah prayed seven times for rain, he received a signal from the eastern sky,—a cloud as large as a man's fist—appeared.

Gideon also provides us with an example, for he too asked for a sign.

And in all the years of my ministry, God always shows me signs in all circumstances. Sometimes I have huge signs but some other times I have very small signs. Big or small, they are God's signs.

Divine Timing

After I have received a sign, then I take the final step: I pray until I know God's timing. God's timing is different from our timing.

You must pray until you have a real peace, for peace is like the chief umpire who has the last word. If, after you pray, you still feel a restlessness in your spirit, then the timing is not proper. That means there is still a red light, so keep praying and waiting. When the red light is not there and you see the green light, peace will come into your heart.

Then you should jump up and go. Go then with full speed with God's blessing and His spoken Word. Miracle after miracle will follow you.

All my life I have conducted my ministry by using these five steps. So far God has confirmed His will with signs and miracles when I take these five steps. Here lies the difference between the written Word and the spoken Word. God's spoken Word, in specific situations, leads us through.

Now you don't need to be confused about the promises of God any longer. No amount of claiming, travailing, jumping or shrieking will convince Him. God Himself will convince you by imparting His faith into your heart.

The English translation of Mark 11:22~23 says that you should have faith in God and then you would be able to command a mountain to be removed and cast into the sea. The Greek version, however, says that you should have the faith of God (Εκετε πιστιν θεου).

Then how can you have the faith of God? When you receive the spoken Word of God, you have received the faith from God. The faith did not come from you. It is imparted faith that God has given you. After receiving this imparted faith, then you can command mountains to be removed. Without receiving God's faith, you cannot do this.

You should carefully study the Bible, from Genesis through Revelation, in order to give the Holy Spirit the material which He wants to work with. Then when you wait upon the Lord, the Holy Spirit will impart His faith to you. Great miracles will follow you as you act on this faith, miracles in your ministry and in your home.

So wait on the Lord. Never consider it a waste of time. When God speaks to your heart, He can in one second do far greater things than you could do in a entire year. Wait upon the Lord, and you will see great things accomplished.

5

The School of Andrew

When you receive Jesus Christ as your personal Savior, you are instantly born again and your spirit is reborn. In that instant the miracle of salvation takes place and God's life is poured into you. Instantly, the new man in Christ Jesus takes control; but your mind and your thoughts must be renewed according to your born again spirit. That task of renewal is one that requires a lifelong process, taking time, energy and struggle. This renewal is necessary if one is to adequately receive and act on the spoken Word he has received from God so that the powerful creativity of the spoken Word will remain vital.

A Renewed Thinking Life

We need to renew our minds in order to truly grasp the thoughts of God. Though many people experience spiritual rebirth, they do not renew their minds. They do not align their personal lives according to the thoughts of God, either. For this reason, God who dwells in them by the Holy Spirit, cannot move freely through the channel of their thinking life. Let me illustrate this more clearly. One day my eldest son, who at that time was in the fourth grade, came to me. I could tell he wanted to ask me something but he was hesitant in speaking. Finally, I spoke first: "Son, what are you trying to ask me?"

He smiled. "Daddy, if I ask you a strange question, will you get mad?"

"Of course I won't get mad," I assured him. "Go ahead. Speak."

"Well," he continued, "are you permitted to tell a lie before your own congregation?"

"When did I tell a lie?" I asked.

He laughed, "I've heard you telling a lie again and again to your congregation."

I was shocked. If my son distrusted me, then who could trust me? "Son," I said, "you sit down and tell me when I told a lie."

"Daddy, so many times you told your congregation that you had heard from the Lord, so I became curious. Every Saturday I would listen outside your study as you were preparing your sermons, and I would open the door a little to see if you were really meeting God there.

"But I never saw you really meeting God in your study. Yet on Sundays you came out to the platform and boldly declared to the people that you met God. And that's a lie, isn't it? Don't be afraid of telling me the truth. I am your son. I won't tell the people."

Since he was so young I knew that he would not understand if I were to explain my feelings in theological terms. "Lord," I prayed, "you must give me wisdom." How can I explain my relationship with you to this young mind?

Suddenly a bright idea came to me and I looked at my son and said, "Son, let me ask you a question. Have you ever seen your thoughts?"

He paused a moment and said, "No, I haven't seen my thoughts."

"Then you have an empty head," I answered. "You have no thoughts at all."

"No, Daddy. I do have thoughts. Because I have thoughts, I can talk."

"But," I pointed out, "I haven't seen your thoughts."

"How can you see my thoughts?" he asked. "They are somewhere in my brain, and you can't see them."

"Well then," I said, "even though you can't see them, you really have thoughts, don't you?"

"Sure, Daddy," he answered.

"Well," I explained, "I meet God even though you cannot see Him with your eyes. God is just like your thoughts. God is a Spirit and those who worship Him must worship Him in spirit. The Bible says that God is the Word.

"Son, What is the Word? The Word is God's thoughts clothed with vocabulary. And if God is thought clothed with Chinese, the Chinese people understand God's thoughts; when God's thoughts are clothed with English, then American people understand them. When God's thoughts come down to us clothed in the Korean language, we Korean people understand.

"Son, I meet God by reading the scripture, the Word of God; and God's thoughts touch my thoughts in the unseen realm and I have conversation with the heavenly Father through the Word. God is just like thought."

Immediately my son grasped the meaning and nodded his head. "I can't see my thoughts, but I still know that I have them. Yes, God is like thought. I can't see God but God is there. I am satisfied. I am sorry, Father, because I misunderstood you."

When my son left I stood up and praised the Lord: "Father, I was afraid that he would not understand, but he did; yet I know it was not I, but the Holy Spirit who helped me to have the words to explain your wonderful presence."

Now, let me ask you a question. What is God like? Does God have a form? Does He look like a human being? How can you explain the presence of God?

God speaks through his Word to your thoughts. If you do not have any thoughts then God has no channel through which to speak to you. You cannot touch God with your hands. You cannot breathe God as if breathing air into your lungs; for God does not belong to the sensual world. You can meet God only through the arena of your thinking life.

God's thoughts come through His Word by the Holy Spirit. His thoughts touch yours and it is there that you meet God. At the time of conversion, your spirit was saved but your soul is not completely changed yet. Your mind is part of your soul and it needs to be renewed.

Many people still live with their old minds even after conversion. The old way of thinking is limited so God becomes limited to them . To walk closely and intimately with God one must renew his mind and his thinking life. Romans 12:2 says, "Be not conformed to this world: but be ye transformed..." How? "By the renewing of your mind, that ye may prove what is that good, and acceptable, and perfect will of God." Renewing the mind is having it transformed by the Holy Spirit as we read the Word and obey it. This means that we should be eager to obey the truth. We must be quick to repent when God

speaks through His Word to us. We must be eager to
have peace with God. James 1:21 adds more to the
above regarding the renewal of our minds: "Wherefore
lay apart all filthiness and superfluity of naughtiness, and
receive with meekness the ingrafted Word, which is able
to save your souls." You must work on the soulish part
of your nature to be renewed, which is necessary to know
God's thoughts. As you renew your thinking, faith will
rise in your inner spirit.

First you must hear the Word of God, since it is
through hearing that the Word of God comes into your
thoughts. Through your thinking life, the thoughts of
God go into your spirit and produce faith. And through
faith great changes begin to take place in your Christian
walk. The life of Christ begins to produce righteousness
and obedience to the Word. Therefore, if you do not
renew your mind after conversion, you will not clearly
understand the power of the Word of God; and without
renewing your mind and hearing the Word, you cannot
have faith.

But as you renew your mind you hear the thoughts of
God. The arena of your thinking engrafts God's thoughts
and they become your thoughts. And God's thoughts in
your heart produces faith. It is through you and your faith
that God plants faith in others. Your thinking life is very
important! You must renew your mind. There are three
steps by which you can renew your mind and these three
steps must be followed before you can achieve a renewed
thinking life.

A Changed Thinking Attitude

The first specific step you must take is to change your thinking attitude from negative to positive. Let us look at Peter, Jesus' disciple, as an example. (Matt.14:22~31)

Jesus' disciples were in a boat on the Sea of Galilee. It was a dark and stormy night and the waves were so high that the boat rolled heavily. They were fighting a losing battle to keep the boat afloat and suddenly they saw someone walking on the water toward them. In those days, there was a popular saying that if a seaman saw a ghost on the sea his boat would sink. So when these fishermen—disciples—saw Christ they were frozen with fear, thinking that their boat was going to sink and that they were going to die.

But Jesus said, "Be of good cheer; it is I; be not afraid."

Peter cried out, "If it be thou, bid me come unto thee on the water."

Peter always spoke before he thought. He was a terribly emotional man; nevertheless, he had the gift of boldness so God used him.

Jesus then told Peter to come. When Peter heard His command, he accepted the command immediately and his thinking was renewed.

Humanly speaking, Peter could never walk on the water. When he accepted Jesus' words, however, his thinking was changed and man always acts according to his thoughts.

The renewing of Peter's thoughts happened so quickly that he probably didn't have the time to consider any possibilities but to go to Jesus! Jesus' words put great faith in Peter's heart, along with great boldness, and Peter jumped out of the boat. It was pitch dark that night. The waves were high. But Peter actually began to walk on the water when Jesus bade him come.

Miracles always follow a renewed mind. As Peter renewed his mind, he had no doubts and he walked on the water! He walked high on the crest of the waves. Yes, he was actually walking on the water!

But suddenly something happened. The Bible said he looked around him. When he looked, he saw the dark valleys the stormy waves had created. Immediately he regressed to his old way of thinking, "Look at me...I am walking on the water," and instantly he began to sink. The Bible says, "For as he(man) thinketh in his heart, so is he...." (Proverbs 23:7) (So will he act.)

This can relate to other attitudes of life too. If you have a low self-esteem, you will act as if you are unworthy and of no account.

It is vital that we renew our minds and think positively. Let me illustrate this point with an actual example.

I once knew a doctor who claimed to be an atheist. For a long time he was a great enemy to my ministry and I suffered much because of him. He challenged my faith and attacked my words and preaching.

One day, that doctor suffered a stroke and became paralyzed. As a result of his paralysis, he was slowly dying. The doctor then came to my church, asking that I pray for his healing.

Many people brag about their atheistic views; yet when they experience a dark night of physical trial and encounter the storms of life, their atheism becomes very weak.

This doctor came to the church and I prayed for him. He received the prayer of faith and stood up and walked from his wheelchair! His steps were strong. All the people clapped their hands and shouted, praising God.

The following Sunday he came to the church again, walking by himself with no assistance. Again he requested my personal prayer; however, I was very busy that Sunday and could not pray for him. When he saw that I could not personally pray for him he changed his thinking. His thoughts regressed to doubts and he lost faith. Because he could not receive a prayer of faith from me, he became unbelieving again and as he walked out of my office to his car, he collapsed. His wife had to call an ambulance to carry him to the hospital. Instead of maintaining faith in Jesus Christ and keeping his eyes on Him, he permitted negative thoughts to take over in his heart and he lost his healing, just as Peter doubted and began to sink. And the doctor became paralyzed again.

A renewed mind should always believe God and take Him at His Word. Your thoughts are important. Continue to renew your thoughts according to the Word of God day in and day out. God is light and in Him there is no darkness. There is nothing negative in Him. Feed your mind with the scripture, for the Word of God is positive and will keep your mind renewed.

Also, be careful when you feed on the Word of God that you do not confine your thinking to traditional patterns of thought only. Dare to believe God for difficult and impossible situations. He is God. He delights in doing great and mighty things for His children.

Be revolutionary. Dare to believe God for greater things and bring glory to His name! Many people are bound because they think only in the traditional and orthodox way, and therefore God is unable to accomplish the great works He desires to do through them. But when you receive the Word of God, your thinking will become revolutionized. Then believe God to achieve great things beyond your present limitations.

When I am in Korea I have a session with my seven hundred fifty associate pastors twice a week. I challenge them, asking them to revolutionize their thinking.

"Don't just think traditionally," I exhort them. "Don't go by the thinking of your own limitations. Go by the Word of God. Feed on the Word of God. Expand your thinking life according to the scripture, then God will have absolute freedom to express Himself through your thoughts."

My associates are highly motivated by my words of challenge. They receive the Word, and if they hit a revolutionary thought, they follow through with it and I see the results. I do not intervene with their work except for those occasions when they experience difficulty.

Once I have delegated authority, that power remains delegated and I no longer worry about it. I work with my associates through this positive approach. Each of these successful ministers is responsible for meeting the needs of a designated number of our 700,000 members.

Think in Terms of Miracles

When you have changed your thinking attitude from negative to positive, your second step must be to constantly discipline yourself to think in terms of miracles. This attitude can be seen in the lives of the disciples of Jesus Christ.

Once, Jesus went out to a wilderness with 5,000 men following Him. Besides 5,000 men there were probably 10,000 women and also many children. In actuality then, there were probably at least a total of 20,000 in this crowd. As the evening approached, it was getting dark and cold and the people became hungry.

Christ called Philip, "Philip, I can see all these people are hungry. Feed them."

So Philip received the command from the Lord Jesus Christ to feed this large crowd. By transferring what happened into modern terms, we can see Philip organizing a group of people what we would call today a "committee," in order to study how to feed this large number of people. Imagine him recruiting the members of his committee, calling together disciples with high intelligence.

Philip opened the committee meeting as chairman, saying, "Gentlemen, our Lord Jesus Christ commanded me to feed these 20,000 people in the wilderness. So our committee has the responsibility to find the way to do so. Do you have any ideas?"

One fellow lifted his hand, and after Philip recognized him, said, "Don't you know we are in the wilderness? We are not in downtown Jerusalem. It's absolutely impossible to even think of feeding these people."

"I think so, too," Philip might have answered.

"Mister Scribe, write that down."

A second man lifted his hand, "Mr. Chairman, I want to ask you a question. Do we have enough money? We would need at least two hundred denari to feed even a small portion of them. Do we have enough money?"

"No," Philip responded, "we haven't got a penny."

"Well, you are out of your mind trying to feed them then," the man retorted.

"Yes, I agree with you," Philip returned. "Mr. Scribe, write that down, also."

The third man spoke: "Mr. Chairman, do you know any bakery that could produce so much bread at once?"

"No," said Philip, "I don't know any bakery around here."

"Well then, it'd take weeks to feed these people, and

that's impossible!"

"Yes, I agree with you," said Philip. "Mr. Scribe, write that down too."

Then another disciple spoke, "I want to express my opinion too, Mr. Chairman. You know it is getting late. Why don't we just scatter them and tell them to each find a place to sleep and eat?"

The meeting was then adjourned, and Philip gathered the information. But this information was only negative and refuted the teachings of Jesus Christ. It directly opposed His command.

Philip then went to Jesus to inform Him, but as he began to speak, Andrew walked up with five loaves of bread and two fish in his hand. "Andrew," Philip may have exclaimed, "are you trying to make fun of us? What are you doing? You have five loaves of bread and two fish to feed 20,000 people! You are really out of your mind!"

But Andrew did not answer him. He just brought the five loaves and two fish to Jesus.

"Jesus, this isn't enough to feed many people, but I brought them to you, anyway."

Andrew heard the command of Jesus. His mind accepted the command and though he may have doubted, he brought to Jesus the food he found. Andrew had possibility thinking and, through his thinking, he caught the vision of Jesus Christ.

Then Jesus blessed that bread and the fish and

multiplied them and that great crowd was fed.

All Christians belong to Jesus Christ; but in Him there are two schools of thought—one is Philip's school of thought and the other is Andrew's school of thought. Unfortunately, many churches belong to the School of Philip, only talking about the impossible. They cry that this is the wilderness and that it is too late, and that the people cannot be fed. They speak with little faith and talk only of the impossible.

To which school do you belong? Do you belong to Philip's school or do you believe that Jesus Christ is the same yesterday, today and forever so you have chosen to join Andrew's school?

When God spoke to my heart in 1969 and told me to build a church that would seat 10,000 people I had mingled feelings. Because the vision had been birthed into my spirit, I was excited and full of new expectations; yet, I was frightened too. At times I felt like Philip and at times I felt like Andrew. I talked with the board of elders and all of them thought like the disciple Philip. They would tell me it was impossible.

When I talked with my 600 deacons (at that time), I found that every one of them thought the same way. So I, too, joined the School of Philip. I went to Jesus in prayer and told Him I could not build that church. As I prayed, Jesus spoke to me by the Holy Spirit, "I did not ask you to confer with your deacons and elders. I simply told you to go and build!"

"Lord," I replied, "you know that I don't have anything

to build the church with. It will take so much more money than I have now."

Little did I realize what His next question would be to me. "What do you have that you personally could give?"

In my heart I knew what He was asking but I refused to recognize His request. "Jesus, don't ask me to do that. I got married when I was thirty years old, and throughout the years I've saved my money so that I could build a beautiful home and give it to my bride. I can't sell that house."

But the Lord replied, "Sell your house and bring that money to me with faith."

"Oh, God, this is terrible!" I responded. "How can I do it?"

"If you are ever to believe my Word and witness my miracles," the Lord admonished me, "you must first be willing to give what you have."

To a Korean wife, home is everything. It is the place she raises her children. It is the place she builds her life. It is a precious possession to her. I was afraid to tell my wife and so I began to travail in prayer. I prayed that my wife would consent with me about the selling of our house.

That evening I brought gifts of flowers and scarves home to her.

"Why are you bringing me these gifts?" She asked. "Are you worried that I don't love you anymore?" But she was pleased at the gifts, and she prepared the dinner happily.

"Oh praise God," I responded. "I'm so happy that I've chosen you. If God ever wanted me to choose a girl all over again, I'd still pick you. You are more beautiful to me each day."

After a while, when I felt it was the right moment, I said, "Honey, I have a big problem."Concerned, she looked at me insisting, "Tell me what the problem is."

"We are going to build this big church that will seat 10,000 people," I said to her. "It will cost five million dollars and as I was praying about this matter, the Holy Spirit spoke to my heart and said that if I was to get the money for the church, I would have to start from my own household first to give. God wants us to submit five loaves of bread and two fish...and those five loaves and two fish are our house!"

My wife turned pale and then looking straight into my eyes she said, "This house is mine, not yours. Don't you dare touch it. It belongs to me and to my children. You cannot give this house."

Her reaction was just as I had expected. Then I went back to the Lord and prayed, "Lord, I've done what I could. The rest is up to you. Send your Holy Spirit to prick her heart so that she will surrender."

That night as I prayed, I could see my wife turning and tossing constantly in her sleep. I knew then that the Holy Spirit was working. I said to the Lord, "Lord, keep on nudging her."

And sure enough the Lord nudged her. For almost a week she could not sleep, and her eyes became bloodshot. Finally she came and said to me: "I cannot stand it any longer. I cannot refuse what the Holy Spirit wants from me. I'll give up the house." So she brought the title deed and gave it for the construction of the new church. We were like Andrew. Though he had only five loaves and two fish in his hand, he had the faith that Jesus could multiply the small portion and make it more than sufficient for the entire crowd. We too, belonged to the School of Andrew.

And so the church plans began to develop. I was glad many many times that the vision to build the new sanctuary came from the Lord into my heart because the days that lay ahead were filled with trying situations. One day a problem came up about the land on which we had planned to build. The Korean government had been developing a special piece of land called Yoido (Yoi Island). This entire property was to be modeled after Manhattan, New York. They were building government buildings on the land and they would allow only one church to be built there. From all over Korea, bids came from the Presbyterians, Methodists, Baptists, Roman Catholics, Buddhists and Confucianists. All applied to the government to build their church or monastery, and I also submitted an application. The man at the application desk looked at me and asked, "What denomination do you belong to?"

"The Assemblies of God," I replied.

"You mean that church where people shout praises to

God in such a loud and noisy way? And pray for the sick and speak in strange tongues?"

"That's right," I responded.

He shook his head, "You know this church is going to be right in front of the new National Assembly. This church must be dignified, and your church is not. We can't accept your application."

In a way, I was happy when I heard his response because this would excuse me from building the church. I returned to the Lord in prayer, "Lord, you heard that, didn't you? We are not dignified enough to build there."

You know, you can bring to the Lord every excuse you can think of but the Holy Spirit always has an answer. The Holy Spirit responded saying, "When did I ask you to go and apply for a building permit?"

"Am I not supposed to?" I questioned.

"My child," He answered, "You must walk the way of prayer and faith and I will lead you what to do next."

So I began to fast and pray. Then in my heart, the wisdom of the Holy Spirit spoke, "Go and find out who is in charge of developing that island."

I went to the Seoul city zoning office and learned that the city's Deputy Mayor was in charge of developing the island. I made a little research on him and his family. I found out that his mother was a member of a Presbyterian Church. So I visited her and prayed with her. One day she became filled with the Holy Spirit. She then began to come to my church.

In Korea, the mother-in-law carries quite a bit of power and authority over her daughter-in-law. I encouraged this lady to bring her daughter-in-law to church, saying, "Your daughter-in-law must be saved!"

So she and I prayed about it. The following Sunday she brought her daughter-in-law to the church. After listening to the sermon, she gave her heart to Christ and later she was filled with the Holy Spirit.

Then I began to work through her to win her husband to the Lord, thinking, "If I've got the wife, I know I can get to the husband." I instructed her, "You've got to bring your husband to the church."

"But he's so busy," she replied.

"You don't want him to go to hell, do you?" I asked sternly. "So bring him to church."

The day she eventually brought him to church the Holy Spirit and I preached a powerful sermon. Though not looking directly at him, the message really was for him and miraculously, he gave his heart to the Lord that Sunday.

The next Sunday he walked into my office. "Pastor, you know I'm in charge of the development of Yoido. We are permitting one Korean church to come and build there. I wish we could bring our church there."

I wanted to shout, but the Holy Spirit would not allow me to. Sometimes the Holy Spirit works in very mysterious ways. The Holy Spirit impressed my heart to say

no, but I argued, "No, I've worked so hard for this."
Though my heart was dying to say "yes," I replied, "No,
Mr. Deputy Mayor. To bring this church to Yoido would
take an enormous amount of money and we would have
to buy at least three or four acres of land. That would cost
more than five million dollars. I think it's impossible right
now. To make matters worse, we are considered to be an
undignified Pentecostal church, and they would not even
accept my application."

He smiled and said, "I think I have a way. You pray
for one week and then I'll come back. You can give me
the answer then, because I can take care of it quickly."

For one week I prayed, and the next week he returned
to my office. "Pastor, if you make the decision to move
the church there, I'll make all the arrangements for you to
have the choicest land. I'll also do all the paper work with
my own office paying the expenses. I'll send my man to
the National Assembly Building to get all the necessary
agreements, and I'll do all the paper work for that too.
More than that, I'll make all the arrangements for you to
buy the land on credit from the city government. I'll do
everything for you and you will have the land."

Then the Holy Spirit said in my heart, "SHOUT!"

"Mr. Deputy Mayor," I said, "I accept."

God would not let me say "yes" for one week, and as
its result, we not only miraculously got the land but we
were saved from doing all the paper work as well!

Then I chose a construction company and signed a
construction contract. Shortly afterward, they broke the

ground, and the construction of the church and the apartment building began. The Deputy Mayor is now one of the leading elders in our church.

Your faith is bound to be tested in similar ways too. If you have a small project, you will be tried in a small way; but if you have a big project, you will be tried in a big way. Never think your faith will take you through a bed of roses. You will go through turbulence by which God will test your faith.

So far, in the construction of the church I still belonged to the School of Andrew, and with great faith I prayed through each new problem.

But then the dollar depreciation came, and the contractor broke our contract. He said they had to renegotiate and he raised the construction cost. Then the oil crisis came. My people began to lose their jobs and the church income decreased so much that I could hardly meet even the interest on the loans. I could not pay the salary of the church staff and I myself received no salary either.

Then the construction company filed lawsuits against me because I could not pay the increased amount. I would come to the church and would receive lawsuit notices, one after another, from the electric company, the sewage company and the construction company. Papers were piled on my desk, yet I had no money to pay any of them. I didn't even have the money to hire my own lawyer. I would sit behind my desk, and one by one, church workers began to leave because I could not give them their salaries. Nobody wanted to stay in a sinking ship and I was sinking fast.

Since we had sold our house and had no place to go, I brought my family to one of the unfinished apartments on the seventh floor of that apartment building next to the church. It was very cold and there was no running water nor heat.

Each evening I would come home to a barren apartment, and all night we would shiver in the cold weather. We had no food and everything seemed so dark. I was hitting rock bottom, and fast becoming a disciple of Philip. I said to myself, "Yes, I made a mistake. I should never have believed God in such a way. I should have thought in the traditional pattern. I should not have started to walk on the water. All this business about faith is a fake. All those voices that I heard in my prayer life must have been the voices of my own consciousness, not from the Holy Spirit. Yes, I made a mistake." And I began to feel sorry for myself.

People were beginning to leave my church and all the reports were negative.

Even my family began to doubt me. Everything seemed impossible and I was tired and hungry. "This is it," I said one day, as I looked out of our apartment window. This is the end. This is the so called life of faith. I am going to finish my life.

"I'm going to jump from this apartment window," I continued, "and I'm going to die. But I don't want to go to hell. I've been working for You all these years, and at least I should get something in return. If hell is worse than this place, why should I go there?

"But I can't live in the world like this. I am going to commit suicide but please accept my soul and let me go to heaven!"

The impact of that prayer was more powerful than I realized and as I prayed, I heard a voice saying, "You are a coward. You want to jump and become an object of ridicule of the people. Will you remain a coward? Or will you be a man of faith?"

"Yes," I admitted, "I am a coward."

Again the voice spoke, "Not only will you go to hell, but you will also pull down many of your members who put their trust in you. You borrowed money from some of the elders and members. Remember the thousands of dollars you borrowed from the precious sisters in the church? They all trusted you. And now you are going to throw yourself down and commit suicide?"

"It will bring about a chain reaction. Because of your cowardice they will lose their faith. They will have broken homes and some will also commit suicide. What a repercussion you will cause the Christian world to feel!"

These words poured into my heart forcefully and brought me to reality. I slumped down crying, "Oh God, then what can I do? Why won't You let me die?"

The Holy Spirit spoke to my heart, "You cannot die. You must persevere. You must see all the debts paid; all the people's debts be cleared."

I stood up, left the seventh floor and went to my office. I knelt down, travailing and crying. News of my desperate state began to spread among the people. Suddenly they experienced a reawakening of faith, including those who had already left the church. "Let's save our pastor," they cried. "Let's save the man of God!"

A "Save-Our-Pastor" Drive began. It was a cold winter and we had no heat, but people by the thousands began to flock onto the ground floor of the unfinished church. They had to sit on rice mats and blankets on the ground, but they came. Thousands of people also began to fast and pray, praying through many nights. They cried out to God, "Save the man of God. Save our pastor! "

Then God began to move. Ladies began to cut their long hair, bringing it to the platform to be sold for wigs. There was an exceptionally touching incident. One day an eighty year old woman, who had no children or no support and who was barely living by the help of the government, came to the platform, trembling and weeping silently.

I knew she had something to say so I listened. She had brought her old banged-up stainless steel rice bowl, a pair of chop-sticks and a spoon. Offering them to me she cried and said, "Pastor, I want to see you delivered from this situation. I want to see you helped, for your ministry has been such a great blessing to me for many years. I want to do something but I have no money. This is all I have," and holding up her old rice bowl, chop-sticks and spoon she added, "I want to give it all to the Lord's work. I can eat out of a cardboard box and I can eat with my fingers."

Everybody's attention was focused on this elderly woman as she spoke. My own heart was melted. "My Lady," I said, "I can't accept this. It's all that you have. You need these to eat your meals everyday. I cannot accept them."

She broke down in tears again, "Wouldn't God accept this gift from a dying old woman? Wouldn't He? I know that this isn't much help to you but I want to give something."

Suddenly one businessman stood up and said, "Pastor, I want to buy that." And he paid nearly $30,000 just for that old banged up bowl, chop-sticks and spoon.

A spirit of sacrifice swept through our congregation and the hearts of the people were melted as never before. People began to give again! Some sold their houses and moved to small apartments. There were young couples who gave their whole year's salary to the church, choosing to live by faith for one year.

This great movement brought results and soon money began to flow in to the church and I could pay the interest on the loan. Banks began to open their doors to me and amazingly, in less than a year everything began to work out. I paid all the debts and was cleared by 1973, when the sanctuary was completed and dedicated. Not only was I able to pay the interest, but I also had the five million dollars to finish building the church and the apartment building!

Again, God proved that the School of Andrew is the best, and to think in terms of miracles is to think as God would have us think.

Many people think that when you have faith, everything will flow easily, and few problems will be encountered. But it is important to remember that it is not so. Think of Abraham. He had faith but he endured trials for twenty-five years; Jacob endured for twenty years; Joseph for thirteen; Moses for forty; and Jesus' disciples passed through trials and temptations all their lives!

Do not be discouraged if you go through a few weeks of difficulty or a few months of trial. Do not throw your hands up in defeat and cry, "Oh where is God?"

God is always there! He is testing you! Sometimes God wants to stiffen and strengthen your backbone and sometimes, while being strengthened, you can almost hear the bones cracking. But if you stand on the Word of God and have faith, God will never fail you!

I once wrote a post-dated check for $50,000, payable on December 31. I scrapped money from every source available, but I was unable to gather even a small portion of the amount. If I had not been able to put the money in the bank by the designated day, the newspapers would have carried a headline saying that the pastor of the largest church in Korea wrote a hot check.

It was twelve noon of the day the money had to be in, and I was still praying. "Oh, Father. I've spent all my money—more than I had. I've borrowed money from many people. Father, where shall I go? I've no place to go."

I continued praying. Then the clock struck one o'clock, then two, and then three. My wife called, "Honey, did you get the money yet? "

"No," I answered.

She said, "Do you know that at four o'clock the last plane leaves Seoul? That's your last chance to escape to America."

"I can't do that. I can't avoid my responsibilities," I said to her. "I can't escape. And if I did, a smear would come to the name of Jesus Christ. I'd rather meet whatever happens here in Korea than escape the country."

The bank was to close at six o'clock, and it was now five. I became desperate. I could not either sit nor stand. I just kept pacing around the office, back and forth, like a restless lion in a cage. Again I prayed, "Oh Father, please come and help me."

Suddenly the Holy Spirit gave me an idea,—that I go to the head of my bank and boldly ask him to write me a check for $50,000. "Father," I responded, "I must be losing my mind. I've overheated my mind's computer and now it's overloaded. I don't have anything to put up for collateral. I haven't even prepared the papers for a loan. You want me to just go and ask him to write me a $50,000 check? This is absolutely out of order!"

But the Holy Spirit insisted, "Yes, I do those things which are beyond man's perceived natural order. You go and do it."

I called my treasurer. "Mr. Park, would you go to the bank with me? I am going to ask the president of the bank to write me a $50,000 check."

He looked at me and then he began laughing, "You have really lost your mind, haven't you? This is December 31. It's five o'clock. You have no appointment and people are lined up to see the president.

"Moreover, we don't have any assets for collateral for a loan. No paper work has been prepared. It's foolish! I'm not going with you. If you want to go, go ahead but I don't want to be a fool with you."

"Okay," I replied. "I'm going with a renewed mind, whereas you are confined in a traditional mind."

I took the car and rushed to the bank. The parking lot was packed, but I managed to park and I walked into the bank.

Humanly speaking, there was no way for me to meet the president. His secretary's office was filled with people. "Dear Holy Spirit," I said, "I've come this far. Please give me more instructions."

The Holy Spirit spoke to my heart, "Walk courageously. Be very bold. Act like a big shot. Don't pay any attention to anyone else. Just walk straight through to the president's office."

So I straightened up, walking through. His secretary noticed me and asked, "Sir, where are you going?"

I looked right into her eyes but said nothing. She questioned me again: "Sir, may I ask who you are? Do you have an appointment? Who are you?"

Suddenly an inspirational thought came to me. "I am from the highest authority." Thinking that I was a special emissary from the President of the Republic of Korea, her attitude changed. She became polite. "You are from the highest authority?" she asked. "Certainly, you may meet him." Then turning to the people waiting she said, "This man must go ahead of you."

She took me ahead of everyone else, straight through to the bank president's office. As I walked in I said, "Dear Holy Spirit, now I've gotten this far. What should I do now?" The Spirit of the Lord was upon me, and just as He had come upon other men of faith, I was made bold!

The Spirit kept repeating, "You are a child of the King, an important person. Keep acting like the big shot you are." So I boldly walked in, sat on the sofa and crossed my legs.

The president walked in. Greeting me with a big smile, and extending his hand, he asked, "What kind of business do you have? For what purpose did you come? Do I know you?" I did not answer his questions, but instead said, "Sir, I've come here with a tremendous project, and I am going to do a great favor for you.

"A favor?" he queried.

"If you will do a small favor for me, then I will give you 10,000 new bank accounts the beginning of the new year," I said to him.

"Ten thousand new bank accounts!" he exclaimed.

"Pick up the phone and call the police. Ask about the name Yonggi Cho, and you'll find that he is the pastor of the largest church in Seoul. He has more than 10,000 members, and also has great authority over his people. He can have all of them transfer their bank accounts to your bank for the new year. I will do this tremendous favor for you if you do one for me."

He called his secretary right away to check what I had said. All the facts cleared as true. He then asked, "What is this favor I could do for you ?"

"You write me a check for $50,000," I said. "I have no time to do the paper work for the loan. But you are a businessman. I am the King's businessman. Many times a businessman enters a huge undertaking with nothing but faith and confidence to show that he will succeed. Small business matters need to go through the law and paper work, but when we make a big deal, we bypass these things and trust that the deal will be successful. If you are a big businessman—and I think that you are— then you will do this for me."

The president called in his vice-president, and the vice president said, "You can't do that. Your neck would really be on the line. It's not just $5,000. It's $50,000 and he has no collateral or no papers. You can't do it."

"If you won't do it," I interjected, "then I have other places I could go. I could do this favor for Cho Heung Bank," which was another large bank in our city.

The man sat down and shook his head. Then he said, "Sir, I feel funny. I've never felt this kind of mixed emotions before in my life. I trust you. If I didn't trust you so much I would never do this. But I kind of like you. You are a bold person and I like your faith. I'll be putting my whole career and life in your hands by doing this, and I'll never do it again. But this time I'll stick my neck out. Bring me a $50,000 check," he instructed his vice-president. "I trust you to keep your promise," he said to me as he wrote out a check for $50,000 from his own personal savings, for a loan to our church.

As I walked out of the office with the check, I felt ten feet tall. Once again I was in the School of Andrew. I turned in the money just as the bank was closing at six o'clock and I was saved.

The following year we transferred all of our church accounts to this bank which the president preferred instead of 10,000 accounts.

So many times God waits until the very last moment to answer our prayers. Once you have renewed your mind and once you have learned how to walk with God, then you must persist to the very last moment in trusting God for this kind of miraculous intervention. Do not be frightened.

Renew your thinking life. Do not be conformed by traditional thinking. Renew your thinking by studying the Word of God. This is the Textbook with which you can renew your mind and be filled with positive thinking and learn to think in terms of miracles.

Orient Your Mind to God's Success

The third step to a renewed mind is to orient your mind to success. You must permeate your thoughts with a consciousness of victory through Christ in every situation. You must orient your thoughts toward receiving God's abundance. God never fails. Every promise has a condition and as you meet the conditions, you may come boldly and ask for whatever you need. So, if you are receiving God's thoughts, you are on the path to successful living in every way.

God never loses a battle for He is the eternal Victor, and because He is the Victor and He lives in you, you should have victory consciousness. God never lacks for anything; and since you are His child and you have oriented your mind to live in God's thoughts, you will have abundance—consciousness and faith will lead you to God's abundance.

This kind of consciousness is important. Think the way as God thinks! There is no negativeness in Him. If you have inferiority-consciousness, poverty-consciousness, sickness-consciousness or failure-consciousness, you have not allowed the positive attitudes of your born-again experience to be yours. You make choices every day in every situation of life. In your Christian life and perspective, you have two choices: to live with negative thoughts or to live with positive thoughts. Your success begins with knowing you can do all things through Christ Who strengthens you. Yes, you can, but the choice in this is yours. The Holy Spirit will never force you to decide one way or another. God is your Help. He is Abundance. He is Life! He is Peace. He is Victory. In Him is only triumphant living. His Word is full of examples that can help you see how success-oriented God really is. If two men do not agree, how can they work together? God has your best in mind for your life and work. So to walk and work with God, you must engraft God's high expectations of you and His success-consciousness into your heart to be your own.

Renew your mind. Constantly read of the men in the Bible who were successful and why. Think in terms of victory and in terms of abundance. When you have completely renewed your mind, you will be a candidate to receive the spoken Word of God. Boldly assimilate the Word of God into your thinking life. Through prayer and reading the Word of God your faith will grow, and through faith, you will be able to lift your chin high.

Look only to the Lord. Though you may not feel anything, live with your renewed thoughts and trust God. Remember that Jesus Christ is the same yesterday, today and forever. Jehovah God never changes. The Word of God never falls on ground without bearing fruit,—without your seeing results.

We cannot live by bread alone, but by every Word that proceedeth from God. It makes no difference if one is black or white, yellow or red or from any of the different races. We are all in the body of Christ and He loves us, no matter who we are. We live by His Word which is always a lamp to our feet to guide us to successful living.

So renew your mind. Constantly think in terms of success, in terms of victory and in terms of His blessing upon your life to give you an abundance in whatever you need so that you can bless others.

Think big with big objectives. You have only one life to live. It is precious to the Lord. He wants to see you bring glory to His name. Since He dwells in your life, all of his triumphant victories can be your triumphant victories.

Christ is still as powerful as He was two thousand years ago but today He works through his redeemed ones. He blesses them so that they can bless others, and so the world can see Him in you and me.

The Law of Thinking—Asking

Ephesians 3:20 reads, "Now unto Him that is able to do exceeding abundantly above all that we ask or think, according to the power that worketh in us..." I call this principle the law of thinking—asking. Many people think that they will receive something by just asking. The Bible, however, tells us He will do more than we can think and more than we can ask. God gives answers through your thinking life, your concept of how big He is or how small your concept of Him is. He does "exceeding abundantly above all that we ask"... above and beyond all that we could ever ask for or think of.

What is your thinking life like? Have you renewed it? God wants to do exceeding abundantly above what you think He can do, but it will be according to the renewal of your thinking life. Do you think poverty? Do you think sickness? Do you think "nothing is possible?" Do you think negatively? Do you think in terms of failure? If you pray with these negative attitudes, God has no proper channel through which to flow because he doesn't live with the negative! Regardless of which country you live in He is your Source! He can do exceeding abundantly above all that you can ask or think—right where you are. He is still the God of miracles! He knows where the resources are. They are all His! The Bible says, "He owns the cattle on a thousand hills" and that is right. If necessary, He can sell some in His own mysterious way wherever you are to meet your needs according to His Word right where you are.

You must read the Bible. But do not read it for your obligation to the Lord or a new rule for living. Do not read it for historical purposes. But do read it to feed your heart and mind so that the Holy Spirit will have material to renew your thinking life. Fill your thinking with the Word of God. Meditate on it as David did. Then you can walk and talk with God in a new dimension and out of your life will flow His miracles and power to touch others and bring glory to Himself.

Seed Faith

What is total faith? How could you have total absolute faith?

It is easy to say, 'believe' but actually to believe without having any doubt in your heart is not easy. My heart grasped a wonderful truth and I want to share it with you.

In Mark 11:22~24 we read, "And Jesus answering saith unto them, Have faith in God. For verily I say unto you, That whosoever shall say unto this mountain, Be thou removed, and be cast into the sea; and shall not doubt in his heart, but shall believe that those things which he saith shall come to pass, he shall have whatsoever he saith."

In my own experience, I labored and struggled to have steadfast faith for years. In many situations, I said over and over, "I believe. I believe!" But actually I could not really do so. In my heart, I did not have the unshakable assurance with peace, which seems to be present only when faith is present. It was a struggle. How could one believe without having any trace of doubt? Is it really possible for one to have faith without doubt in his heart? If you can really believe with all of your heart without a bit of doubt then you could command your mountain to be removed to yonder sea and the mountain will move. But if you command your mountain to be removed yet if it doesn't move, that is an indication that you still have doubts and struggles and that you don't have total faith. A mountain will move only when one has total faith.

Jesus said, "Have faith in God." When this verse of the scripture was translated, the Greek scholars translating this verse together, discovered that it could have two different meanings. One group translated it, "Have faith in God." The other group translated it, "Have the faith of God." Though they translated this verse in two different ways, those Greek scholars said that both translations are accurate.

Let's look at this more closely. From the Greek trans–

lation, we see that God actually put two meanings together. Therefore, they must never be separated from each other. We must combine them and keep them together. We must have faith in God and we must also have the faith of God in us.

Faith first begins with our own human effort to believe. It is often a struggle to try to have faith in God. We don't have the peace we desire and we are concerned that we don't have peace. Nevertheless, even though it is a struggle to believe, it is the beginning of a faith foundation.

In Mark 2:1~5, we read about a paralytic man who was totally helpless. He may have received many kinds of treatment, yet he could not get well. One day he heard the news that Jesus Christ was in his town and he believed if he could go to Jesus he would surely be healed. He believed with all of his heart but just believing did not bring healing. Then he decided to put action to his faith. He asked four of his friends to take him to Jesus. Placing him on a stretcher, the friends went to the place where Jesus was. As they arrived, the crowd was so great that they could not even get close to the door. But he was determined to get to Jesus, and a determination always finds a way, so they discussed taking him to the roof of the house. Climbing to the top of the house, they uncovered some roof tile. They broke just enough to let the man on the stretcher down exactly in front of Jesus.

The Bible says as this was happening, "Jesus saw their faith." Yes, Jesus actually saw the paralytic's faith and spoke directly to him, "Son, thy sins be forgiven thee." (Luke 5:20) "I say unto thee arise" and immediately the paralytic rose up before them... and departed to his own house, glorifying God." (vs. 25)

What was the difference between the first and the second phase of the paralytic's? In the first phase of faith, the paralytic came believing. Yes, he really believed but nothing happened. Jesus saw his desire to be healed and his determination to get to Jesus and He saw that the determination would drive him to do all he was able to do from his part to get to Jesus.

Something interesting and powerful happened here. When Jesus saw the faith of the paralytic, THEN He imparted His miracle working faith on the faith of the paralytic. At the very instant, that very moment, the sick man experienced a mountain moving miracle! There is a very important principle of truth here,—your faith brings the faith of God.

Jesus wants to see our faith in the daily circumstances of our lives too. As believers, we desire to have growing faith. We desire to see miracles happen in our lives.

It is important to know that every believer has faith in God. At the time of conversion, faith is born into the hearts of believers by the Holy Spirit. But to experience growth in faith, we must use it. By exercising faith for smaller things, our faith will grow to believe God for greater things and draw the faith of God until a mountain moving miracle is experienced. God always works with our faith.

The first stage of our faith is a struggling faith or human faith. Although it is a struggling faith, it still is faith in its first stage. Then one must plant "seed faith" to exercise more faith and to bring about the miracle needed.

Albert Einstein discovered the Law of Relativity in Physics and made it known to the world. Dr. Oral Roberts advocated the "seed faith" as the most important principle in receiving the faith of God. "Seed faith" is a seed which is to be released to show your faith to God. God wants to see your seed faith. You may say, "I believe! I believe! I believe!" but God says He wants to see the proof that you really believe. Even though you struggle, God can see faith through your struggle and He wants to you to show the proof that you believe. He desires you to show your "seed faith". When He sees the proof of your faith, your seed faith, He will impart His faith on your faith and perform miracles for you!

The paralytic showed his faith by doing all within his power to go to Jesus. How do you show your faith? Can He see your faith? He is looking for your faith on which to bestow His faith so that you will have the mountain moving faith. Many people exert human effort only, hoping by their own power to make a miracle happen. The principle of the Word of God is very clear here: when the paralytic demonstrated his will to do all that was humanly possible to get to Jesus, by his persistent and determined total effort, then Jesus saw his faith that he would be healed. Don't try to receive a miracle by your human faith alone. Human faith is only human faith. It is the first stage faith and it needs more to touch the heart of

God. God wants to see your seed faith. Human faith, the first stage of foundational faith, alone cannot remove mountains but when you plant the seed faith, your human faith will move toward greater faith that will move the heart of God for a miracle.

Seed faith is very important. When I have a great problem, though I believe that God can solve the problem, I always want to show my faith by doing all I am able to do. Although I believe, I also bring seed faith to God in the form of a large amount of monetary offering, which at times is a sacrifice for me. Sometimes I tremble in my heart, "My God, can I survive giving this much seed?" But I bring my seed and sow it in God's work. Then I continue to pray and wait in God's presence until I hear from Him in my spirit. Sooner or later God's faith comes upon me and when it does, I know it! I can rise up and command my mountain: "Mountain, be removed from my place to yonder sea!" And the mountain always moves. Hallelujah! Have you had a mountain removed? Have you planted seed faith that God can see?

One of my elders had a son who was slowly withering and dying with rheumatoid arthritis. I prayed for him everyday, "God, healing is in the scriptures. You promised to heal. I believe that you will heal him. I do believe!" But when I laid my hand on the boy to pray, I struggled to have faith. That boy was never very far from my thoughts. I believed but I did not have the faith of God for his total healing. Though I prayed for him for three years his condition gradually became worse. Finally he became completely crippled and could not walk at all. Members of his family carried him on their backs to and from school. The parents were millionaires but they had never sown seeds into the Kingdom of God. They only brought their son to me for prayer. They earnestly desired him to be healed and I tried to exercise my faith for him but my heart remained full of doubts. Three years later, this family decided to sow seeds into the Kingdom of God. They brought a large gift to church to present to the Lord. Then they continued to pray with me for his healing.

One evening while my elders and their wives were having dinner in our church dining hall with my wife and me, I was thinking about the boy again. Though I had prayed every day for three years for that boy, suddenly that evening during the dinner, the Spirit of the Lord came upon me and God's faith came into my heart for his healing. Suddenly I could believe the total healing of this child with absolute unwavering faith. I began to tremble in my heart. So great was the power that came upon my heart! I had no doubt or fear that he would be healed. That was really great faith. Until that time, I had had faith in God for healing in general but this time I recognized again God's supernatural faith had been given to me and, as awesome as it was, I knew I was believing the boy's healing with God's faith. I stood up and walked to the table where the boy's parents sat. Standing before them, I announced, "Elder Kim, tonight your son will be healed." As I spoke, I knew without a doubt that the painful mountain of rheumatoid arthritis would be removed. Seized by such great faith, I repeated, "Tonight, your son will be healed. Go home in peace."

As I spoke, this fine elder and his wife began to cry. Soon there was not a dry eye in that room because we all had shared the suffering of this family and had prayed for their son too.

As I returned to my table, my wife asked what I had said to make the family cry. I told her I announced that the son would be healed that night. My wife was upset. "You prayed for the child for three years and nothing happened; but now you suddenly told them that he would be healed tonight. What if he isn't healed? The word will spread and what will happen to you?"

Her response was a normal reaction from one who had not received with the faith of God for healing. But I knew he would be healed that night. The witness of his healing came to me instead of the parents this time, though they had sown the seed of faith instead of me and though we both had faith.

What happened to change the course of the child's physical condition? They went as far as they could to show their faith to God, to show that they were believing Him for healing of the son. They sowed seed. God saw their struggling faith and mine but now that they had shown their faith by planting seed, God had imparted His faith. Now, I not only had faith in God, but the faith of God came upon my faith and I recognized it.

That evening as the parents returned to their home, the son crawled to the door as usual to greet them. After exchanging questions and comments, the parents spoke to the son, "Pastor Cho came to our table during the dinner and announced that you will be healed tonight and the manifestation of that healing will be seen tonight. Son, in the name of Jesus stand up."

The boy began to cry. "Daddy, you know I can't stand. I've been crippled for three years and I forgot how to stand."

"Though you think you forgot, son, in the name of Jesus and on the authority of His Word, we command you to stand up." The presence of the Lord was very real in that room that night. Everyone was crying and worshipping the Lord at the same time. Then taking the hand of the child who had become twisted and helpless for three years, they patiently assisted him and let him make the effort to stand. Suddenly the supernatural began to happen. The twisted legs began to straighten out before their eyes! He stood on one foot, then pulled the other one up and as he acted in faith to pull himself up. The miracle working Holy Spirit healed the boy completely so that he could walk. Slowly he walked outside and down the street. Neighbors heard the commotion and came out to witness the most unusual that they had ever seen. The Healer had come! The faith of God had been demonstrated again and the boy was healed completely that night.

The healing of the crippled child became an incredible testimony in that neighborhood because the entire neighborhood had seen his condition for three years. Now, they were astonished as they saw him begin to jump around and later walk to school by himself. From everywhere, people asked, "What happened to him? What happened?" Thanks to this miracle, many non-Christian neighbors turned to Christ and Christians were greatly encouraged. They learned a valuable lesson, the importance of planting seed.

In 1987 the Lord led me to begin publishing a weekly and daily newspapers covering both secular and Christian news. It is our "silent preacher" to our nation and to other countries where the Korean people are living.

A few years ago, I needed a 40 million dollar loan to purchase a high speed printing press from Switzerland. I needed the money within two weeks, but I didn't have the equity to borrow that much money. I had all the faith in the world in God but my faith was in the stage of a struggling faith. One moment I really believed. The next moment, I had doubts in my heart. I had many sleepless nights. Yes, I believed but my faith was not total faith. I did not have the faith of God. I could not command this mountain to be removed to yonder sea. Then, one day I made a decision to sow seeds for the glory of God.

"Oh God," I prayed, "I only have foundational faith, my human faith, but now I have sown my faith seed. Now I am waiting for you to do your part."

I continued to pray one week. By the end of the second week the contracts had to be completed. On Thursday my treasurer came to my office. "Pastor, we will not be able to get a Letter of Credit from the bank. We don't have the equity they require so they will not lend us the 40 million dollars. Furthermore, they said that in the seventy-year history of their bank they had never issued a loan for that amount of money without equity."

In my heart I knew this mountain would be removed. "I have faith in God," I told my treasurer, "but I don't have the faith of God yet. At any moment the faith of God will come upon me because I have already sown my seed."

Thursday evening, after returning home, I went to my prayer closet as usual. I began to pray again. "Oh God, I've sown my faith seed to you. I know you will help me!"

After praying, I was waiting quietly in the presence of God and in an instant the heavens seemed to open and God's faith came upon my heart and upon my faith. I recognized it. I began to receive God's faith! When God's faith comes you will surely know it! Indescribable peace came and settled all over me. Fear was gone. In a few seconds, I felt like I had received all the faith in the universe. I stood to my feet and with authority, I spoke out loudly: "Bank, I command you to issue that Letter of Credit for 40 million dollars."

As I came out of my prayer closet, my wife recognized immediately that my face was glowing and instinctively she knew what had happened. The next morning I went to the church and called my treasurer: "Go to the bank. The Letter of Credit will be issued today!"

"Pastor," he exclaimed, "You are a dreamer!"

"Yes, I'm a dreamer," I said. "Yesterday my dream had only foundational faith but I received the faith of

God. This mountain shall be removed. I commanded it to be removed and it will be removed."

The treasurer went to the bank. He was there three or four hours but when he returned, he had a Letter of Credit for 40 million dollars! That was the result of the faith of God!

Some time later, the president and officers of this bank visited me. They seemed a little nervous. "In the seventy-year history of our bank," they said, "we have never issued a Letter of Credit for that amount of money without equity. However, we felt as if we were compelled by a higher power to lend you this amount of money and we're glad to do it."

The faith of God! There is a distinct difference between human faith and the faith of God. First, faith begins from the human side and it is a struggling faith. But the scripture invites us to have faith in God because it becomes a beginning faith. With this beginning faith, we can proceed to receive the faith of God. How can you receive the faith of God? By doing all you can do to show God the faith you do have,—by sowing seed—then stand on His Word. When you sow seed you will have made a foundation for God to place His faith upon. Can you see this truth?

After sowing your seed, then pray and wait. The waiting period is very important. Without doing it, don't launch out by your faith alone. Believe and worship God. And when His timing is right, He will put His faith on your faith. He will speak His Word to you and the faith of God will be manifested.

Yes, the paralytic man had faith but he needed more faith. So he went further. He sowed seeds of faith by his actions. He did all he could possibly do to get to Jesus. Would you allow anyone to go on the roof of your house and to break up the tile or roofing to make a hole large enough to enter if you would not be compensated for the damage? This guy really believed and demonstrated his faith by planting seed. He probably said in his heart, "I will pay for the roof later but right now no matter what it costs to get to Jesus, I must get to Him!" And he must have promised to pay for the repair. It is the faith that Jesus is looking for. How does He know you have faith? How do you show Him your faith? When he sees your seed faith, He will place His faith on yours!

Today you can experience mountain moving faith! God has given 8,000 promises in the Bible for us to use while we are on earth. When you reach heaven you will not need them but you do need them now. To believe God for the promises He has given you, how will you show your faith? Persist to do all you can to show God that you believe. Plant seed! For many years, even fervent believers did not experience many of their mountains being removed because they did not know what it meant to present seed faith to the Lord. As you grasp this wonderful truth, sow your seed. Wait before God until you receive His faith and you too will be able to witness your mountains being removed!

7

God's Address

When we become Christians, not only do we need to renew our minds according to Romans 12:2, thinking positively and thinking in terms of miracles, but we also need to know our Source of power and enablement.

The Confusion

In 1958, after graduating from a humble Bible School,

like every student else, I went out to pioneer my first church. It was in a poor slum area of suburban Seoul. I was neither equipped nor trained for that kind of ministry. In less than three months, I ran out of sermon subjects and I had nothing more to preach.

You might easily say, "Well just go out and speak of salvation every day." But one cannot speak of nothing but salvation day in and day out. To prepare one sermon I spent the entire week searching for sermon topics from Genesis to Revelation. I had summaries of all the books of the Bible but I couldn't come up with one single sermon. I almost felt that I was not called into the ministry because it was too difficult for me to prepare any more sermons.

The poor people in my area were not too much concerned about heaven or hell. They lived from hand to mouth each day and were more concerned about daily survival. Often they didn't know where their next meals would come from. They had no time to think of their future. Wherever I went, these people asked me to help them with rice or clothes or money to build a shack to live in. But I was no better off than they were. I, too, was living in a shack and often I too had to skip meals. I owned only one suit. So I had nothing to give them.

I was in a devastating situation in those days, and although I knew that God had all the resources, I did not know how to touch Him and tap those resources. At times I felt I was near the Lord and touching Him; but the next day it seemed that I was completely out of touch.

So many times I was so confused that I wondered whether I was really walking and living in the Holy Spirit. Many times I would pray, "Lord, I know that you are in my life through the Holy Spirit." Yet, after having a difficult day, when I tried to pray in the evening, I could not sense His Presence so I felt I was completely out of touch with Him. I was confused. I would pray, "Father, it seems that I am in and out of my Christian experience because I cannot always sense You near. I don't know how to stay by Your side or keep You by my side." I wondered where God really was. And so this began a very real struggle in my heart to find the permanent residence of God.

Oriental people, in particular, require the address and location of the god they worship. Most of them grow up under the influence of heathen worship so they need the address of their god in order to go and worship him. When I needed my god in heathenism, I would go to a temple and kneel before an idol. There, I could address myself to him directly. In heathenism every one has the address of his or her god or gods.

But when I came into Christianity, I could not locate the address of our Heavenly Father God. In those days, it was a great trouble to my heart while I was learning the Christian way of life. In the Lord's prayer we would say, "Heavenly Father." But when I meditated on this I would wonder, "Where is heaven?" Then I would reason, since the earth is round, to those who live in the north hemisphere, heaven is to the north ('up'). Then would heaven be to the south ('below') of those who live in the south?

So whenever "Heavenly Father" was mentioned, I was confused. "Father, where are You?" I would ask. "Are You there? Here? Where? Father, please give me Your address!"

When Orientals come into Christianity they have a real struggle because they, too, wonder about the address of God. Many new believers would come to me and ask, "Pastor Cho, give us at least some picture, or even an image, to address to. You ask us to believe in God but where is He?"

In the early days of my ministry I would only encourage them, "Just speak to the Heavenly Father. I don't know His address or location. Sometimes He comes to me and other times He doesn't. I don't know where He lives."

I would often cry alone in the stillness of night about this because I felt I could not continue to preach like that. I needed an answer and so in my own way I started seeking the "address" of our God.

In my imagination, I thought, "If I could go to Adam I would ask him, 'Adam, I am sure that you are our forefather. I know that you would know the address of our Heavenly Father. Please tell me His address.'"

Then I imagined Adam would probably very gladly tell me exactly what I had read in the Bible, "He dwells in the Garden of Eden. If you go there, you will find Him."

Then I thought of the scripture that Adam sinned and fell from grace and he was removed from the garden.

"When you fell from grace, Adam, you were removed from the Garden of Eden. What is the address of the garden?"

Adam would reply, "Well, I guess I don't know."

I then decided in my imagination if I could visit Abraham, he would surely know. "Mr. Abraham, you are our father of faith and you met God often. Will you please tell me the address of our Father God?"

In my thoughts again I could imagine Abraham would reply, "Well, whenever I needed God, I put up an altar and I killed an innocent animal, and I waited upon Him. Sometimes He would meet me and at other times He wouldn't. So I don't know His address."

I left Abraham and continued to visit the patriarchs in my thoughts. Then I came to Moses and said, "Mr. Moses, surely you know the address of God the Father. You had fellowship with Him continually."

"Of course I know Him," Moses would probably have replied. "He was in the tabernacle built in the wilderness. Remember? During the day He was in the pillar of cloud and He was in the pillar of fire at night. You just go there and you will meet God. That's His address."

But in my spirit I reasoned, "When the Israelites came into the land of Canaan, you no longer had the tabernacle of the wilderness. Where is that tabernacle of the wilderness now?"

"It's not there in that same place," Moses answered.

Again, still searching in my heart and mind, I came to

King Solomon. I said, "King Solomon, you built a magnificent temple with colorful granite stones. Do you know God's address now?"

"Of course God dwelt in the wonderful temple of Solomon," he said. "When a curse or sickness spread in my country, people would pray to God Who dwelt in the temple, and in His mercy He would listen to them and answer their prayer."

"Where is that temple?" I asked. "That temple was destroyed six hundred years before Christ by the Babylonians. We don't have the address of the temple now."

"Well, you're right," Solomon said. "That temple was destroyed so I don't have the address of God."

I thought of John the Baptist. "Mr. John the Baptist, surely you know the address of God."

"Yes," John replied. "Look to Jesus Christ, the Lamb of God, who carried away the sins of the world. He is the address of our God!"

Something within my spirit quickened. Yes. Yes! Jesus is the address of God. Through Jesus, God spoke and revealed His love for all mankind. Through Jesus, His only Son, He performed miracles. Wherever Jesus dwelt, there God also dwelt and still dwells!

I rejoiced greatly in my heart that night for the revelation that had come to me by the Holy Spirit!

Then another question came. Jesus died, was resurrected and ascended into heaven; so where is the address of Jesus Christ now? Once again, the Holy Spirit spoke into my spirit.

The Address of God

God always delights to reveal Himself to the person who is honestly searching for Him. God, by the Holy Spirit, came to me with His Word, "Know ye not that ye are temple of God and that the Spirit of God dwelleth in you?" (I Cor. 3:16) What an awesome revelation to my heart that night! Gradually, other scripture verses began to speak to me!

I began to see that God the Father and God the Son dwell in me through the Holy Spirit. In II Corinthians 1:22 I read that God sealed us and gave us the Holy Spirit right in our own hearts. I found that His address is my address! He's in my heart. He is not in the Garden of Eden. He is not in a temple made with human hands. He is in my heart and life!

I went back to my congregation and began to preach that I had found out the Spirit of God dwells in us! His address is our hearts. His address is the heart of every believer who has been cleansed by the blood of Jesus and He dwells in us with all of His power, authority and resources. He goes with us wherever we go. He abides within us.

"He dwells within us. His address is your address," I added to them. "If you stay in your home, He is there in your home with you. If you go out to your place of business, He is there with you. If you work in the kitchen, He is in the kitchen with you. God dwells within you and His resources are found in you."

"Brethren," I continued, "silver and gold have I none. Food, rice and clothes have I none, but I have something to give you. It is the true message that God dwells within every one of you believers. Those of you who have not received Christ, come to Him; receive Him as your personal Saviour; and the great Creator of heaven and earth, with all of His resources will dwell in your heart too! He will supply all of your needs." Upon hearing this message, they began to grow in their Christian faith.

That was the actual starting point and the foundation stone of my ministry. Until that time, I was desperately trying to catch God. When famous evangelists came, I would rush to hear them to be able to touch God. Sometimes I would go to a mountain to pray, and sometimes to a valley. I was searching everywhere to find Him and hold on to Him, but when I found this truth, I did not have to wander any more!

I am able to tell my people, "God is not a million miles away! He is not the God of two thousand years ago! He is not just the God of the future! He dwells within you and He is the God of NOW. His address is your heart! You can talk to Him and pray to Him and commune with Him from your heart. He is closer than your hands or feet. You can touch Him by faith. You can tap His resources through prayer and faith. When you cry aloud to Him, He listens. When you speak to Him softly, He listens. When you meditate, He still hears, for He dwells within you. He has promised to supply all your needs."

After the Korean War, missionaries came to Korea to work for the Lord, and I used to attend the Executive Committee Meetings. Most of the Korean ministers would present all kinds of different projects in those meetings such as the construction of churches or the operation of the Bible college. Among themselves they would discuss the various ways that could bring them solutions. But each time the matter of finance came up, immediately they would say, "Let a missionary come and take over." They used the missionary just as a financier.

I became aggravated in my heart and asked, "Why do you always turn to the missionaries?"

They replied, "God supplies only through the missionaries, not through us."

However, from the time I graduated from Bible School I was determined to have God my absolute resource. I found out that my God was dwelling in my heart, with all the resources I needed. I discovered how to tap those resources and throughout these thirty-six years of ministry I have never depended upon any other resource.

I have crossed the Pacific Ocean more than two hundred times to minister in foreign countries, and I have never asked for a penny from a single church. I would express my appreciation for the sending of missionaries to Korea, but I have never asked for financial help from foreign churches.

I have depended upon God every time and, in every difficult situation, He has supplied every need,—building the church, sending out missionaries from my church to other countries and building the Bible college.

When we built our new Korean Assemblies of God Bible College our church gave over half a million dollars. God indeed supplies our needs!

The Challenge

I want to impress upon your heart the fact that you have all the resources you need within you right now, not tomorrow, not yesterday, but right now. You have the mighty God dwelling within you by the Holy Spirit with all of His resources to bless you for every need you will ever have from now until you go to be with the Lord. He is in your life and circumstances. He is there to work out your salvation; but He wants to work through you. God places a vision in your heart and then He causes you to return to Him for His help. You are the channel through whom He works.

You may pray, "Oh Father, please work mysteriously in the universe and do everything that everyone needs." But God will reply, "No! I have given you my Word. 'You ask and it shall be given...' Be specific and then you will know of my love and power when you see my hand extended to you. If we did not ask specifically, we would never know whether God answered nor would we have the joy of experiencing His specific love for His children individually. He has chosen to work through His children according to His Word, which instructs us to "ask" individually.

You are the channel. You have the responsibility to make your requests known to Him. If you believe that God can do greater things, then ask Him for greater things. If you don't, you do not acknowledge God as the Lord of all authority and power. So do not limit Him even in your thoughts. This is one reason some believers come into His presence and receive many more answers to prayer than other believers.

When people come to my church and receive the Lord, the first truth I teach them is that God is dwelling within them and that they have all the resources they need in Jesus Christ. Then I re-educate them to discipline themselves to work and walk with God. By doing so, their faith grows and they lead miraculous and victorious lives.

If these people had remained poor and were filled with failure-consciousness, how could they have given more than twenty-five million dollars to our church from 1969 through 1990? Every year we have carried out projects ranging in cost from one and a half to two million dollars. These members have given because they have been enriched and they have become tremendously successful. They have been born again, cleansed from their sins and they have understood what the Word of God has taught them concerning righteous living that pleases God. The name of Jesus Christ has been glorified through their lives and God has honored them by answering their prayers!

Most people have personal battles with four kinds of sin of the flesh that must be conquered before they are able to be blessed by God. Without being cleansed of these sins, their lives, their "channels," would be so clogged that the Holy Spirit could not answer their prayers. These are four things I have discovered from my thirty-six years of ministry and by counseling with people.

The Sin of Hatred

People suffer in many ways from hatred. If hatred is hidden in the heart and is never dealt with, God does not flow through you by His Spirit. Sin separates us from God, no matter whether we consider it a small sin or a large one. If the Word of God says it is sin, it is sin! Hatred which often stems from an unforgiving spirit, will be the number one enemy to your faith life. In Matthew, Jesus pointed out, "For if ye forgive men their trespasses, your Heavenly Father will also forgive you: But if ye forgive not men their trespasses, neither will your Father forgive your trespasses."

Usually I do not meet anyone after preaching in the fourth multiple service on Sunday mornings because I am very tired. If someone does come to my office he will first have to go through my secretaries who carefully screen them. If someone finally does reach my door, then I know he must be in great need.

One Sunday after I had preached in the fourth service, a man knocked on the door of my office.

When I opened the door, he walked in with a staggering step. I thought he was drunk. He sat down and pulled something from his pocket. It was a sharp dagger and I was frightened. I thought, "What are these girls doing, letting this man in here? Here he is with a dagger and they let him in without knowing it was in his possession."

I was really frightened, and as he handled the dagger I prepared to defend myself. Then I said, "Don't use that knife. Tell me why you came."

He replied, "Sir, I am going to commit suicide. But first I am going to kill my wife, my father-in-law, my mother-in-law and everybody around me. My friend advised me to come and attend one of your services before I do all these things, so I attended the fourth service. I listened intently but I couldn't understand one word because you were preaching with such a strong southern provincial accent. Since I could not understand you, I am going to go now and carry out all my plans.

"I am constantly coughing. I am a dying man. I have tuberculosis."

"Calm down," I urged him. "Sit here and tell me about yourself."

"Well," he started, "during the last stage of the Vietnamese War, I went out as a technician and bulldozer operator. I worked at the front lines making bunkers and roads, risking my life in order to make more money. I had sent almost all the money to my wife that, when the war was over, I scarcely had enough funds to come out of Vietnam.

"I sent her a telegram from Hong Kong that I was coming home. But when I arrived at Seoul Airport expecting to see her with my daughter, I couldn't find even a shadow of them. I thought perhaps they had not received my telegram so I rushed home and, to my surprise, I found strangers living there.

"I found out that my wife had left me and she had run away with a younger man. She took all of my savings and had moved to another part of town. I went to her and begged her to come back to me but she told me adamantly that she would not return.

"I went to my wife's parents' home and protested. They gave me forty dollars and insisted that I leave their premises. In less than a week I had a burning hatred in my heart and I began to vomit blood. Now, tuberculosis is fast eating away my life and there is no hope for me. I am going to kill myself but first I'm going to destroy everyone of them."

"Sir," I said to him, "this is not the way to carry out your revenge. The best way to get yourself healed is to find a new job, make a better and more beautiful home, and show yourself off to them. In this way you can really carry out revenge; but if you kill all of them and yourself, it would not bring any satisfaction."

"I hate them," he cried.

"As long as you hate them you are going to destroy yourself," I said. "When you hate, you destroy yourself more than you destroy others."

"Why don't you try to believe in Jesus?" I asked. "When Jesus comes into your heart, all of the power of God comes and dwells within you and will flow through you. God will touch you, heal you and restore your life. He will help you to reconstruct your life and that would be real revenge against your enemies."

I sent him to prayer mountain. There, he accepted Jesus Christ as his personal Savior. But still he could not totally forgive his wife. I asked him to bless his wife. "The best way of forgiving your wife is to bless her: bless her spirit, soul and body. Pray to God that He will open the door of heaven with every blessing for her."

"I can't bless her!" he exclaimed. "I will not curse her, but I cannot bless her."

I answered, "If you don't bless her, you will not be healed. When you bless, the blessings start from you and go out. You are going to be more blessed by your words of blessing than she is. In Korea there is an old saying, 'If you want to smear the face of others with mire, you will have to smear your hand first.' If you curse your wife, the curse will flow out of your mouth first. But if you bless you wife, the words of blessing bubble up from your heart, first going through your mouth to bless you. Go ahead and bless her."

He had been standing up. Now he sat down and began to bless her, grinding his teeth. He prayed, "Oh Lord, I bless...my wife. Bless...her. And...give her salvation. Oh God, give her...a blessing."

He kept on blessing her and in less than one month, he was completely healed from tuberculosis and he became a changed person. The power of God began to flowing out of him and his face shone.

When I met him a month later, he excitedly said, "Oh Pastor Cho, I rejoice in the Lord! I praise God that I can say I have a real appreciation for my wife. It was because she had left me that I found Jesus! I pray for her every-day. I have renewed my license as a bulldozer operator and now I have a new job. I am making a new home and I'm waiting for my wife to come back."

This man was praising the Lord. His life was being restored through the power of God as it flowed out of him because he had been healed in spirit and body. Unfortunately, his wife never returned to him. Some time later he got married again and he and his new family continue to live victoriously as they attend our church.

Without getting rid of hatred, you cannot really get in touch with the Lord. In your ministry for the Lord, you must help people realize this.

One day a principal of a school came to see me. She had been suffering from arthritis. She had gone to many doctors at many hospitals but they could not help or cure her. I laid hands on her and prayed, rebuked the arthritis and shouted but God did not touch her.

Many people had been healed in our church but in spite of much prayer, she was not. I began to feel like giving up. But one day the Holy Spirit said, "Don't shout, pray and rebuke. I do not flow through her with healing because she still hates her former husband."

I knew that she had been divorced ten years before, but as she was sitting there I said, "Sister, please divorce your husband."

She looked at me and said, "Pastor, what do you mean, 'divorce your husband?' I divorced him more than ten years ago."

"No, you didn't," I replied.

"Oh yes, I did," she insisted.

"Yes," I replied, "of course you did legally. But mentally you have never divorced him; you are still living with him. Every morning you curse him and hate him and that hatred is destroying you and drying up your bones. Because of this, you cannot be healed of your arthritis. No doctor could cure you."

She retorted, "Oh, but he did such harm. When we were married he never got a job. He used all my income. He messed up my life and then he left me for another women. How could I love him?"

I replied, "Whether you love him or not is your business. I'm telling you if you don't forgive him you are going to die from arthritis. You can be healed from arthritis only by the power of God. The power of God will never fall down from the sky like a meteor and touch and heal you.

"No!" I continued, "The Holy Spirit, the Healer today, is dwelling within you and He desires to rise up with His healing power within you; but you hinder the flow of His healing power with your hatred. Begin to bless your former husband. Bless your enemy and do good to him. Then God's love for him will grow within you and the hatred will go. God's love for him in you will create a channel through which the Holy Spirit will flow with healing and touch you."

She had the same struggle as the man with tuberculosis did. She began to cry. "I can't love him. Pastor, please forgive me. I will not hate him, but I just can't love him."

"You can't stop hating him if you don't allow the love of Jesus to come in a positive way in your heart to love him," I replied. "In your heart, look at your husband; touch him and tell him that you love him and bless him."

Once again she struggled so I led her in a prayer. She cried, gritting her teeth. But eventually she began to feel love for him and prayed. She asked God to bless and save him and give all the good things to him. The power of God started flowing in her and she was touched. In less than three months she was fully delivered from her arthritis.

Yes, God is dwelling in you by the Holy Spirit. But if

you have hate and you do not rid yourself of that arch enemy, His power cannot flow through you to heal you.

The Sin of Fear

Many people live under fear. It is our responsibility as Christians to help them to release it in the name of Jesus. Fear is the second sin of the four.

I had always lived under the fear of contracting tuberculosis, and one day I did. When I was a student in a junior high school, I took a science class, dealing with bottles of alcohol filled with bones and intestines. The sight of these things frightened me.

One morning our biology teacher was teaching on the subject of tuberculosis. He said if one ever contracted tuberculosis he would become dissipated and his insides would look like the intestines and bones in these bottles for the rest of his life.

He told us of the dangers of tuberculosis and concluded his lesson by saying, "There are people who are born with a tendency to have tuberculosis. Men with narrow shoulders and long necks seem more apt to catch tuberculosis."

All the students began to stretch their necks out like cranes and as I looked around I noticed that I had the longest neck in my classroom. Right away I knew I would get tuberculosis. Fear struck me and when I returned to my room I stood before the mirror looking at my neck all afternoon. In those days, there were no miracle drugs. Then fear came into my heart and I began to live every moment with the thought that I would surely get tuberculosis.

At 18, I contracted tuberculosis. Like attracts like and like produces like. If you have fear then the devil has an open channel through which to come and strike you! Fear is negative faith. So, the thing that I greatly feared came upon me. As I feared tuberculosis, I contracted tuberculosis; and as I vomited blood I said to myself, "Yes, this is exactly what I expected."

I read a claim in a Korean medical journal that many Korean people die from habits. I thought about this and wondered, "How can people die from a habit?" Then I read on the article.

These non-Christian doctors wrote that fear plays a strong role in our lives. For example, suppose a man died from high blood pressure in his fifties. When his son was in his fifties, he also died of a stroke. Later the grandson lived in fear of dying of a stroke.

When he reached his fifties, the moment he felt a dizziness in his head he thought, "Oh, a stroke is coming. I am ready." If he felt something in his chest he would wait momentarily for a stroke, each day living with this fear and expectation. Fear creates this situation in his body, and soon he will expect to die of a stroke.

Many women die because of the fear of cancers. One woman might say, "Well, my aunt died of cancer, and my mother died of cancer, so I'll probably die of cancer, too."

When she reaches an age similar to that of her aunt and mother at the time of their deaths, and if she experiences any type of pain, she will probably say, "Oh, this is cancer. It certainly is coming now." Everyday she will wait, saying and thinking to herself that she is going to have cancer, repeating this over and over. It was in this way that the doctors said people were dying from "habits." If a person has a specific fear, then the power of destruction will begin to flow.

In 1969, when God asked me to move from my second church and to build our present sanctuary, I had 10,000 members with a constituency of 12,000 people who attended regularly. I was happy, feeling good and satisfied. I had a good home, a wonderful wife, three sons, a beautiful car and even a chauffeur. I responded, "God, I'm going to stay at this church until my black hair turns white."

But one day while I was praying in my office, the Holy Spirit spoke, "Cho, your time is up here. You must be ready to move."

"Oh, Lord," I said, "Move? I already pioneered one church and this is my second pioneer work. Do you want me to pioneer again? Why should I pioneer churches constantly? You are choosing the wrong person. Go to someone else," and I started arguing with God.

No one should ever argue with God for He is always right. Eventually God persuaded me, saying, "You go out and build a church which will seat 10,000—a church that will send at least 500 missionaries."

"Father," I replied, "I cannot do that. I have always dreamed of building a large church but suddenly I'm scared to death of building a church like that."

But God said, "No! I've told you to go. Now go!"

I calculated roughly with a contractor about costs. He told me that we needed two and a half million dollars to build a church that size; another half a million dollars to put up an adjacent apartment complex. So I would have needed five and a half million dollars at that time, in 1969.

The contractor asked me how much I had. I told him I had $2,500. He gave me a blank look, shook his head and did not even comment.

Then I went to a meeting of our church elders and told them about the plan. One elder said, "Pastor, how much money are you going to raise in America?"

"Not a penny," I answered.

Another elder asked, "How much money can you borrow from an American Bank?"

"Not one penny," I replied.

They said, "You are an excellent minister but you're no businessman. You can't build a church and an apartment building like that."

Then I called the 600 deacons that I had at that time. I told them about the plan, but they immediately began to act like scared rabbits, as if I were levying a high tax on their lives.

I became discouraged. Full of fear, I came to the Lord, "Lord, you heard every word the elders and deacons said. They were all in agreement that it couldn't be done, so you've got to think this over again."

Then the Holy Spirit spoke clearly and forcefully in my heart, "Son, when did I ask you to go and talk with the elders and deacons?"

"Am I not supposed to?" I asked.

The Holy Spirit answered, "I commanded you to build the church, not to discuss it. That is my command."

I got up from my knees and said, "Yes, if it's your command, then I will do it."

Through a series of miraculous events we were able to secure one of the choicest pieces of land on Yoido. Then I went to the contractor and made a contract to build both the church and the apartment building complex on credit. I thought to myself, "They will build the church easily. I will trust God and see."

After the ground breaking service I went out to look around. I thought they would just dig a few yards down and then put up the building. But when I looked, there were dozens of bulldozers, digging into the earth as if they had planned to develop a lake! The cavity was enormous!

I almost became crazy with fear. I asked, "Father, do you see how they're digging? And I have to pay for all of this? Oh, I can't." And I became frozen with fear. My knees trembled and in my imagination I saw myself being carried away in a prison van. I knelt down again and prayed, "Oh, God, what can I do now? Where can I go? Where are You? I know that You are the total Resource and I put my trust in You! I surrender my fear to You."

When I prayed, I could envision God's workings and my spirit became calm. My fears went away; but when I looked at the situation again, I struggled with fear again. So for the duration of the construction I lived with my eyes closed more often than open.

This same principle is true in many situations. If you look at your circumstances from the human standpoint with your physical eyes and live by your senses, Satan will destroy you with fear. But if you close your eyes to the human circumstances and look only to God, then you can believe. The Holy Spirit will keep His encouragement in your heart!

There are two different kinds of knowledge—sense knowledge and revelational knowledge. We should not live by our sense knowledge but should live by God's revelational knowledge found in the Bible from Genesis through Revelation.

We should teach people to surrender the fear of their surroundings and their circumstances. If they do not commit their fears to the Lord, they cannot develop their Christian faith nor can the Holy Spirit flow through them. Ask them to surrender their fears to the Lord and teach them to put their faith only in the Word of God.

The Sin of Inferiority

Many people live with an inferiority complex and are constantly frustrated. This feeling of inferiority is the third problem area I will discuss.

If people feel that they are inferior because they live in a slum area, you cannot pull them out easily. Perhaps they failed in their businesses and have resigned themselves to being a failure. As long as they have the failure complex and attitude, you cannot help them. They must face these problems, surrender their inferiority complex to the Lord, and then you must help them to be confident in life through the love of God.

There was a Korean family with two sons of elementary school age. The parents had loved the younger son very much and continually praised him in the presence of his older brother. Eventually the older brother began to feel unloved and inferior. One day, the parents were away from home and the boys knew it. Returning from school, the older brother killed his younger brother with a knife. It made a sensational news topic in many homes. It was all brought on from an inferiority complex. A sense of inferiority can slowly become very destructive and must be dealt with.

After pastoring two years in my first pioneer work, my church was growing steadily. It was truly a noisy Pentecostal church. People were being filled with the Holy Spirit and many were being healed. One day the Executive Committee of my denomination called me in.

At that time, they stood somewhere between being lively Pentecostals and staid Presbyterians.

The committee members questioned me, "Are you really praying for the sick and getting people to shout and speak in other tongues in your services?"

"Yes," I replied.

"You are a fanatic," they asserted.

"I am not a fanatic. I am doing everything according to the teaching I learned in Bible College," I defended myself.

After discussing my pastoral methods, they took my ministerial license and kicked me out of my denomination. When I was removed from their ministerial fellowship I was struck with feelings of inferiority. Feelings of fear and destruction also tried to take over my life and I had a difficult struggle. Soon after that, missionary John Hurston came to Korea and brought me back into that denomination.

When the members of the Executive Committee had put me out, little did they realize that one day I would become the General Superintendent of our denomination and I held that position for ten years. When I was first elected to that office, our denomination had only 2,000 members. By applying the laws of faith and teaching them to the pastors, we experienced rapid growth. At the time of my resignation from that position, our denomination's church census revealed a total of 300 churches with more than 200,000 members.

We must help those who feel that they are unable to conquer life. We must pull them out of their depression an pessimism. We must build them up in faith and in the love of Jesus Christ, assuring them again and again that nothing is impossible when we put our trust in God. We must heal them and train them. By and by, with our help and the help of the Holy Spirit they will rise up out of their inferiority feelings.

One Sunday morning as I was preaching in the second worship service, I saw a man brought in with his hands and feet bound. I knew this man was mentally sick. That particular day we were making pledges for the fifth stage of our building program. People received pledge cards and filed them. When a pledge card was handed to this man, I noticed that he received it and with his bound hand, he wrote in one hundred dollars.

His wife laughed when the deacon came again to receive his card. "Don't believe him," she said. "He's not mentally responsible."

But after the service I met him and found out that, to my amazement, he had been completely healed by the power of the Holy Spirit that morning during the service! He was in his right mind and he talked with me. He told me he had been suffering severely from an inferiority complex. "I had owned a fertilizer factory," he began, "but I failed and went heavily into debt. I worried so much that my mind snapped. My family took me to an institution and there they gave me all kinds of shock treatments. But none of them helped me.

"But as I was sitting here listening to your sermon this morning, I suddenly came out of my deep depression sickness and recognized reality. I've lost my friends, my prestige, and my credit. I have a mountain of debts. I can do nothing. I am nothing, but I'm so grateful that I experienced God's healing today!"

"You are something," I said to him. "You are not inferior. Since you came to Jesus now all of the power of Christ and His resources are dwelling within you. You are going to be used by God. You are not inferior because you are God's man. Stand victoriously. You have all of God's power and resources dwelling within you, just waiting to be tapped," I continued.

"What kind of job am I going to have?" he asked me.

"I don't know," I replied, "but keep on reading the Bible and pray, and you'll know."

One day he came to me, filled with excitement. "Pastor, I read the verse of scripture that says we are the salt of the earth. How about my going into the retail salt business?"

"If you believe in it," I said, "go right ahead. Do it!"

So he went out and began to sell salt on a small scale. He paid his tithes, paid his pledge and continued to rejoice in the Lord. God began to bless him and his salt business grew and grew. A few years later, he built a large storehouse right beside the river where he placed fifty thousand dollars worth of salt.

It was summer, and one night it rained heavily into the

early hours of morning. I got up that morning and found out all of the area had been completely flooded. His storehouse also was flooded and I was concerned. That afternoon when the rain stopped, I rushed out to his store.

Other articles and materials can still be found after a flood but salt has a great friendship with water. When I entered his warehouse, there was no salt left. But the man was sitting in the middle of his warehouse, singing and praising God. As I walked in, I tried to discern whether he was in his right mind or not. I went up to him and asked, "Are you okay?"

"Pastor, I'm all right," he smiled. "I'm not crazy. Don't worry. I've lost everything, but as you always told me, I have all of God's resources within me. Water may have taken away my salt, but it could not take away the total resources or the presence of God dwelling within me. I can tap those resources again and again by prayer and faith. You just wait. Give me time and I'll rebuild my business again."

It was evident he was not suffering from an inferiority complex any longer! He was full of confidence. The Holy Spirit had truly done a great work in his life!

This man became an elder of my church. He is a multi-millionaire businessman in the salt business. He also started a watch company. He has accompanied me to many foreign cities in my missionary trips.

This man is a glowing testimony and example of how people can be helped to release their feelings of inferiority through preaching the Word of God and stressing that they have all of God's resources at their disposal to tap for their needs.

The Sin of Guilt

Many people also suffer from feelings of guilt. It is the fourth problem that needs to be overcome before the Christian can work actively with God; for as long as someone suffers from guilt, the guilt will also hinder the flow of God's resources flowing through him. We need to help people release their guilt feelings. We need to stress to them that when they feel unworthy and full of guilt they can simply come to the Lord and He will cleanse and forgive them and then they will be able to forgive themselves. Then healing will come.

One day a beautiful couple came to my office. The man was quite handsome and his wife was very lovely. Though this lovely wife was in her early thirties, she was so emaciated that she could hardly open her eyes.

The man spoke first, "Pastor, my wife is dying. I have done everything I know to do. I have taken her to doctors of psychology, psychiatry and internal medicine. I'm a rich man and I've spent thousands and thousands of dollars on her but no doctor has been able to help her. Now, they have given up. I've heard that you have really helped many people to be healed."

I told him that was true. I looked at the wife searching

and waiting for the discernment and wisdom she needed in this situation. Silently, I prayed, "Father, now that she has come here, what can I do?"

Right away the still small voice of the Holy Spirit spoke, "She is suffering from a psychosomatic sickness. This is not an organic problem; this is an emotional problem."

I asked the man to leave the room and said to the woman, "Lady, do you want to live? You need to live for your husband's sake, at least. If you were going to die you would have died before now. However, you have three children and if you were to die you would really mess up all of their lives. So, sink or swim. You really have got to live for your husband and your children."

"I want to live," she said to me.

"Then I can help you only on one condition. You must open up your past life," I answered.

She straightened up and with anger glaring in her eyes, she said, "Am I in a police station? Are you a dictator here? Why do you ask that? This is not an interrogation and I don't have to open up my past."

"I can't help you then," I replied. "However, for the sake of your husband and children, I can ask God to directly reveal the past problem areas of your life to me."

She was frightened and taking out a handkerchief from her purse, she began to cry. After a long contemplation with a sigh she said, "Sir, I will open up my past life. But I don't think this is the trouble."

"Yes, it is," I said. "This is the cause of your problem."

"My parents died when I was young," she began, "and I was practically raised in my elder sister's home. She was like a mother to me and her husband was like a father. They took care of me wonderfully, and I lived with them while attending junior high school, high school and college.

"When I was in my third year of college, my elder sister went to the hospital to give birth to her youngest child. During that time, I took care of her home and children. Without recognizing what was happening, my brother-in-law and I fell in love with each other.

"I don't know exactly how it all came about, but we fell into an immoral relationship and then guilt really pierced my heart. From that moment the guilt was so heavy I felt I was going to die. But my brother-in-law continued to call me from his office and I met him at motels, hotels and resort areas.

"I went to the hospital and had several abortions and even then I could not refuse his requests. My brother-in-law continually intimidated me that if I did not comply, he would tell my sister what was happening between us. I was scared to death and I felt I was slowly being destroyed. I felt I had to keep it a secret.

"When I graduated from college I determined that I would marry the first man who proposed to me. I found a job and a young man, who is now my husband, asked me to marry him, without asking any questions about my past. I accepted his proposal so that I could get away from my brother-in-law. I married him and in time my husband became quite prosperous. He resigned from his former job and started his own business. Now he is well off. We have a good home, money—everything.

"But since that affair with my brother-in-law, I have been suffering from these strong feelings of guilt. Whenever my husband makes love to me I feel like a prostitute. I feel I have no right to receive his love. Inside I am torn and crying. My children are like angels and they love me and hug me, but I hate myself. I know that I am a prostitute. I am not worthy to receive this kind of love from my children. I don't even like to look at my own face in the mirror. That's the reason I cannot attire myself in the proper way. I've lost my appetite for food and have no happiness or joy in my heart."

"You must forgive yourself," I said to her. "I have good news for you. Jesus Christ came and died on the cross for you and your sins."

"Not even Jesus can forgive my sins," she cried. "My sins are too big and too deep to be forgiven. I've done everything. Everyone else can be forgiven, but not me! I've deceived my sister and I can't confess to her what I've done. That would mean breaking up her whole life."

Silently I meditated but prayed, "Oh Lord, how can I help her now? You've got to help me."

Then I listened a still small voice within my heart and suddenly I got an idea.

"Sister, close your eyes," I instructed her, also doing the same thing myself. "Let's go to a very quiet and beautiful lake. Now you and I are sitting beside the lake, and there are many pebbles. In my hand I hold a very small pebble. You please pick up a big rock. Let's throw this pebble and the rock into the lake.

"First, it's my turn. I have the pebble. I am throwing it in the lake. Did you hear the sound it made? A ripple. Where is my pebble now?"

She answered, "Well, it went down to the bottom of the lake."

"Right," I replied. "Now it's your turn. Throw your rock in. Yes, you throw it in...Okay, now that you've thrown it in, did it make a light noise?"

"No," she asserted, "it made a big sound and a large ripple."

"But where is your rock?" I asked.

"At the bottom of the lake," she replied.

"Well, it seems that both your big rock and my small pebble went to the bottom when they were thrown in. The only difference was the sound and the ripple. Mine made a plot, yours made a boom. Mine made a small ripple, yours made a large ripple. People go to hell with small sins just as well as big sins because they are without Jesus Christ. And what is the difference? All sin is sin, small or big. Everyone needs the forgiveness of Jesus Christ. The blood of Jesus cleanses away all sins, big and little."

This touched her heart and she woke up to the truth. "Does that mean that my sins could be forgiven by God?"

"Of course," I replied.

She slumped in her chair and began to cry uncontrollably. The truth had reached her heart. I tried to encourage her and cheer her but she continued to cry and cry. Then I laid my hand on her and led her in the sinner's prayer.

When we had finished praying, she looked up and I could see her eyes were shining like stars. The glory of God began to shine from her face. Peace and forgiveness were evident. She stood up and exclaimed, "Pastor, I'm saved! All my burdens are gone!"

I began to sing and she began to dance! Before this time, she had never danced for joy before the Lord but this day she jumped and danced, making quite a noise. Hearing the commotions her husband rushed into the office. She rushed to him and hugged his neck, something she had never done before, and her husband could hardly believe it.

"What have you done to her?" he asked.

"God has performed a miracle," I answered joyfully!

"You must give your whole life to the Lord," I said, turning to his wife. "The Lord has done great things for you." In a very short time she was completely rid of all the guilt and healed by the power of God. It was a tremendous testimony of deliverance and healing.

That couple now attend my church and whenever I look at the wife's face I cannot help thinking of the love of Jesus Christ and how completely it heals. When she let go of her clogging sin of guilt, the power of Christ flowed throughout her body and healed her completely.

Dear Brothers and Sisters in Christ, as Christians you too have all of God's power dwelling within you right now. You can tap that resource for your tuition, your clothes, your books, your health, your business, everything! When you go out to preach the gospel you are not preaching a vague objective, a theory, a philosophy or human religion. You are actually teaching people how to tap the endless resources of Jesus Christ Who dwells in you. You are giving them back to Jesus and He is touching your world through you.

God's Rest

Worry and fear are two of the most powerful weapons of Satan. I know, because I have lived through the pioneering stage of my church to this date often with worry and fear. Many a night I could not sleep. At times I almost felt that I was going to have a heart attack because the oppression was so heavy.

Hebrews 4:10~11 states: "...For he that is entered into his rest, he also hath ceased from his own works, as God did from His. Let us labor therefore to enter into that rest, lest any man fall after the same example of unbelief."

This scripture has great truth and power. Many people are dying prematurely because of worry and fear.

Several years ago, I was having meetings throughout England. I was in a small town by the name of Worcester near Birmingham and I had originally planned to rest on Wednesday. However, a pastor in that town had a heart-attack and I was invited to preach at his Wednesday evening service so that he could rest. At the conclusion of that service, the pastor then asked me to go to the home of one of his deacons to spend the night. I usually prefer to stay in hotels for several reasons, so I tried to talk my way out of staying in a home. I assured the pastor I had money, but he insisted his deacon had a prophet's chamber and besides, there was a need in that home. In a few minutes, a lady came to me, grabbed me by one arm and commanded, "Let's go!" I was a little frightened so I hesitated, "No, no, thank you anyway, but I wi' stay at a hotel tonight." But the lady literally pulled me, nd I had no choice but to follow. She was driving a small Volkswagon. Throwing my suitcase in the back, she ordered me to get into the car so I obeyed, and she drove away. As we arrived at her home later, she told me her husband was still working but would be home by ten o'clock. "Go to the second floor and change your clothes into something more comfortable," she ordered me, "and then come into the kitchen. I will prepare some tea." When preparing dinner, they speak of it as preparing "tea." When I returned a few minutes later, instead of preparing tea or dinner, she was crying.

I came in and sat down and she began a long story. "Pastor," she cried, "I am so sorry to insist that you come to our home but we have a great problem and we cannot solve it. The reason I persuaded my pastor to ask you to stay with us tonight is because we are at the point of bankruptcy. I want you to pray for us."

She continued, "I met my husband during World War II while he was a serviceman in Germany. After the war, I returned with him to England and now I am a naturalized British citizen. We have failed in one business after another. Now, our home is all we have but it is mortgaged also. If we do not pay the mortgage for this home, we will lose it too. The situation is terrible. We have worked and prayed so hard, but God is not answering our prayer. Satan has worked hard to destroy us through our finances. What can we do, Pastor? How can we solve this problem?" she asked between sobs.

I felt compassion for this family so I asked her to get her Bible. "Open to Genesis, the first chapter," I said. "Begin to read and answer the questions I am going to ask you." After reading a few verses, I stopped her and asked, "On the first day, did God create Adam and Eve first and then say to Adam, 'I'm very busy so you must come and help me. Let's create the whole universe together.' Is that what God said in the Bible?"

"No," she responded. "On the first day God created light."

"Did He make the light alone, by Himself?" I asked.

"Yes."

"That's strange," I continued. "Are you sure He didn't need any help? On the second day, read on. What did God make? Didn't He need any help from Adam and Eve on the second day?"

"No," she answered again. "On the second day, God created the firmament and divided the waters above the firmament and called the firmament heaven."

"That's very strange," I said again. "It was surely very tiring for Him to create the whole world by Himself. Surely He would need help from Adam and Eve on the third day. Did he ask them to help on the third day?"

Again she read from the scriptures, "On the third day God commanded the earth to be separated from the waters and commanded all fruit bearing trees to appear."

Then looking at me with a questionable expression she asked, "Does your Korean Bible say that God needed help from Adam and Eve?"

"No," I answered. "My Korean Bible reads exactly the same as your Bible."

"Then why do you ask me these questions?" she asked with a puzzled look.

"I will answer your question after you have read all of chapter one. On the fourth day," I continued, "Did God create Adam?"

"No," she answered, "On the fourth day God created the sun, moon and stars by Himself."

"By the end of the fourth day," I said, "Surely He would have been so tired that He needed to create Adam and Eve to help Him finish His work of creation."

"Well," she read on, "On the fifth day," the scripture says, "God created every living creature that moveth in the water and every winged fowl after his kind, but God never asked Adam and Eve to help him."

I was waiting for her to come to that conclusion.

She continued, "Finally, God made Adam and Eve and made them according to His image."

"When did this happen?" I asked.

"After He had created everything, then He made Adam and Eve," was her answer.

"If I were God, I would never have created the worlds that way," I said. "I would have had them work together with me all through the week. But God did it differently. He created everything by Himself. When everything in His beautiful world was finished then He created Adam and Eve and rested. The seventh day was Adam's first day."

I continued with the main issue I wanted her to see in the spirit, by faith: "Suppose Adam and Eve came to God and said, 'God, this is our first day of life. Everything is so beautiful but isn't there anything I can do to help you?' God would have said, 'No. I finished everything for you! This is my rest day. Your life began on my rest day. I planned and made you to enter life on the rest day. You were not created to work but to live! Now, you are to rest in me!'"

I continued. "Suppose your mother planned an elaborate party for you and you went to her home to help. In the kitchen many gourmet dishes were attractively prepared and ready for the party! You went to the living room but the room was already decorated and the seating arrangement was already completed for the guests. You went outside to the garden and the tables were set with silverware, dishes and arrangements of flowers. Even a special honor seat was already planned for you also. You could see there was nothing to be concerned about because everything was finished just as your mother had said. Even if you had asked a second time what you might do to help, her answer would still have been the same because there was nothing to add to her completed work. She had planned for you to just rest and enjoy her finished work."

I continued to speak to the deacon's wife. "God has finished everything for you too, so why do you try to take His work out of His hands to manage by yourself? The work belongs to God. Work is His privilege. You must not take it from Him or you will mess up His plan. As far as God is concerned, the problem you are facing now was taken care of before the beginning of the world. The Bible says that by the seventh day God had created everything, even this problem that you are facing now. Your burden belongs to God! He already knows how He will solve it, but in His time. Jesus said, 'come unto me all ye that labor and are heavy laden and I will give you rest.' (Matt. 11:28)

"We really commit a sin by trying to take God's role. If God had needed your help, He would have created you on the first day to work with Him. But He never asked anyone to help Him. He has already completed the details of this problem. He finished working it out for you. He has solved all the problems that you will still face in this life. He cares about you! He cares about this problem! To know how He will solve things today and those which will come in the future, we simply must ask Him to show us His way. If there is something you must do, He will show you. Then just obey what He has planned. If He does not speak to you, leave it with Him. If God would have expected you to help Him, He would have created you on the first day to work with Him. He has never asked anyone to help Him, so just obey Him as He directs your life. God's purpose in creating mankind was to have fellowship and communion with man; and for man to enjoy living with Him. The scriptures remind us, 'Seek ye first the kingdom of God and His righteousness and all of these things (the answers to your problems and answers to the tangles of life) shall be added unto you.' (Matt. 6:33)" She listened intently. Now she was looking past me into the truth I had just shared. She began to understand. I paused for her to grasp all of it.

"Why are people working so hard, sweating, worrying and anxious?" I asked her. "Let's recall the story of Adam and Eve. In the beginning they enjoyed a wonderful life because everything had been prepared before God placed them in His beautiful garden. They just enjoyed their surroundings and worshipped God when He came down in the cool of the day to commune and fellowship with them. How wonderful that must have been! What a beautiful beginning for them in their new world! God commanded only one thing. 'But of the tree of the knowledge of good and evil, thou shalt not eat of it for in the day that thou eatest thereof thou shalt surely die.'

"They were privileged to enjoy all the fruit, but they were forbidden to eat what God had said they must not eat,—the fruit from one tree that would enlighten them to the knowledge of good and evil. When we paraphrase those words, we imagine God said, 'You may enjoy all the fruit but you cannot eat the fruit that gives the knowledge of good and evil. That knowledge is mine. That is the symbol of my authority.' God's authority and man's obedience to His authority was the issue here and the forbidden tree represented God's authority. God said that if they ate of that tree they would die.

"Why did God give such a severe command to Adam and Eve? Only the master has the authority to make this kind of a decision. In this case the issue would be their knowing which is good and which is evil. God wanted them to remain in the state in which they had been created: to enjoy communion and fellowship and rest in Him. Yet he placed the tree in the garden and forbade them to eat it so that they would have to choose to obey His authority.

"In Korea, I am the master of my home. I have supreme authority over everything and I decide between good and evil for my family. When my children were small, they always came to me and asked for permission to do certain things. I made the decisions and gave my answer. There were no questions asked and there was no negotiating to change my decision. In those days, my three sons obeyed well, but as they grew older and faced worldly exploitation of many friends it was a struggle for them to obey. I am still the master of my home, but as they became older they wanted to question me and challenge me. They began to insist on having their own independent sovereignty so we had many heated arguments. This same thing happened in the Garden of Eden.

"God is sovereign over all of His universe. No one can challenge Him. As His children, we should remain as children and not try to become masters. We should never exert our own choice of making decisions about our life's difficult problems without conferring with Him regarding what is good and what is not good when God's Word has already given us, 'Seek ye first the kingdom of Heaven and all these things shall be added unto you.' Honoring Him as Master of all of life's situations brings us into His rest!

"Adam and Eve tried to become sovereign themselves by choosing to do what they wanted to do. So they ate fruit from the forbidden tree, and from the moment of their disobedience, they lost their God-consciousness and gained self-consciousness. They lost their power to do good and gained the power to do evil. Now, instead of becoming like God, they became unlike Him.

"God has the power to do only good, always. Adam

and Eve lost their sinlessness and innocence the day they sinned and their spirits died. Eternal death took effect immediately when they disobeyed and their bodies began to decay. (Rom. 5:12~21) They were cast out of the garden and had to take care of their own lives. While they were under God's protection, He took charge and provided everything for them. When they declared independence by their disobedience, God said from that moment they must pay the price of earning their own living by the sweat of their brow. And they began to live by their own human strength. They thought they were sovereign but in reality they became slaves to sin. They tried to live peaceably but enmity and hatred ruled in their family. They wanted to be healthy but disease came to them and began to destroy their health. They tried to live abundantly but thorns and thistles had sprung up. Working to till their ground was not easy. The price of taking authority and becoming sovereign over their lives brought guilt, sickness, curse and poverty. It was anything but rest.

"But the story does not end there. Jesus came! He came to take our sin and guilt, sickness, curse, poverty and the sting of death. He willingly went to the cross of Calvary. His flesh was torn. His blood was shed, because He purposed to redeem man back into a rightful relationship with God. While he hung on that cross, Jesus never asked anyone to come and help Him. Jesus, Father God and the Holy Spirit worked alone to accomplish salvation. Jesus paid all of the debts! Now once again we may come to God. Some people come to Him asking 'God, what must I do to be saved?' God says, 'Nothing my son, I have done everything for you and there is nothing more to be done! You are going to live in my rest. I finished the work! Now, I invite you to come and start to live the spiritual life that I prepared for you. Your part is to trust me. Worship me. Follow me. Rest in me. By my grace, my son, you are saved.'

"If you would try to purchase salvation by your own good deeds you would be usurping Father's sovereignty because the work of salvation belongs to God. That's His privilege. All the religions in the world are abominable to God because they try to work out man's salvation instead of accepting God's freely given salvation. No human religion can save our souls.

"Despite your wretchedness and sinfulness, if you come to God through Jesus, you will receive salvation and be totally saved at that moment because salvation is a gift from God! Grace is grace, not work! We are to live by His grace.

"As far as physical and material things are concerned, God finished all things when He completed the creation. This is not my word but God's Word. Hebrews 4:11 says 'the works were finished from the foundation of the world.' So the material world was completely created from the foundation of the world.

"Spiritually, the work of salvation was completely finished 2,000 years ago at Calvary. Then, the Bible says, 'He that is entered into His rest he has also ceased from his work as God did from His.' God has no more work to do! The physical world was finished at creation. God has no more salvation work to do, either, because salvation was finished 2,000 years ago at Calvary! It is all finished!

"God has ceased from His work, and the Bible says you also have ceased from your own work.

"If He has ceased from His work, what is our part as believers today? The Bible says, 'Let us labor therefore to enter into that rest, lest any man fall after the same example of unbelief.' (Heb. 4:11)

"Everyday we are laboring and we are praying and we are hearing sermons for the one reason: that we may be able to enter into God's rest."

I said to the lady, "See, all through these years you didn't understand correctly that God's work was finished and you must only rest in God and trust. You tried to help God solve the problems of your life. God is going to do it by Himself and receive all the glory for Himself. He will not share His glory with anyone. This is the reason your striving and prayer did not move God. Perspiration brought on because of anxiety is a symbol of the curse. You must repent of your sin of anxiety. You must rest in Him!"

We prayed together, "Oh God, we tried to take the role of God. This burden is Your privilege. You wanted to do this work all by Yourself so You would receive all the glory but we dared to add to Your finished work. For this sin, we repent! Forgive us. Today, we surrender this urgent need to You. We surrender all of our burdens to You. From tonight, we are going to believe You, worship

You, love You, and enjoy Your gift of life without worrying. We are going to rest in You."

As we finished our prayer, she jumped up. "Oh, I feel so free, so totally free now! I am unshackled! I didn't understand this before, but now I do. I'm not going to try to solve my problem alone."

Her husband walked in as we were talking. "Oh," she began to tell him, "I heard a wonderful message from Dr. Cho when we returned home from church. You must hear it. Dr. Cho, please tell the same story to him."

By that time, I was so hungry that I insisted that she tell him the story but give me something to eat.

The next day I left for Cardiff, Wales, where I was having a two-week long revival. I wondered how God worked for this fine family but in a few days I received a letter from the deacon's wife. Instinctively I knew her letter contained good news and it did. She wrote, "Dear Pastor, after you left, my husband and I were living on cloud nine! Your message was exactly what we needed. We began to envision that our burdens already had been taken care of by God, and He was in charge. As we began to rest in Him, one day a couple came by and saw our 'for sale' sign in the yard and came in to see the house. The wife seemed excited and remarked, 'Oh, this is exactly what I've been looking for.' They offered a price which was far higher than we had hoped to receive and the home was sold quickly. The bank was paid and we were delivered from our predicament by the help of God."

You who are troubled, weary, worried or heavy laden, do you really know the meaning of Christ's invitation, "Come unto me?" He invites us, "Come unto me, all ye that labour and are heavy laden, and I will give you rest. Take my yoke upon you, and learn of me; for I am meek and lowly in heart: and ye shall find rest unto your souls. For my yoke is easy, and my burden is light." (Matt. 11:28~30) This verse is filled with comfort for people of all walks of life.

In Palestine many years ago, when a farmer trained a young calf to plough, he placed the young one under the yoke of the mother cow so the yoke was actually upon the neck of the mother. By this way, the younger one learned to plough without any strain on its body. At first it appeared to be hesitant to be placed in a yoke but later it appeared playful and happy because it really it was not carrying the weight of the yoke.

The Word of God never stated we should take our own yoke. His Word clearly says, "Take my yoke..." He would remind you, "I went to the cross. I am pulling your load. You don't have to pay the price for sin. You don't have to suffer. You don't have to pay the price for your problems. Come under my yoke and then you will have rest."

Yes, the yoke is Christ's not yours.

The yoke was made to fit Christ. You are invited to take His yoke upon you and you will find you are not carrying the weight of the yoke. He is! You are to live in His rest, not by your own work! How blessed it is to live in His rest!

If I had not learned this truth long ago, I might have died long time ago. With 700,000 church members, there are weddings, funerals and sick people to pray for—everyday. There are 350 missionaries and often their children are ill and the telexes begin to flow to my office. I must oversee our Elim Welfare Center also, our national weekly and daily newspapers, give TV and newspaper interviews and see that the cost of these things are taken care of. My telephone rings day and night even though I have 750 associate pastors. As all of these needs come to me, it would be easy to fear and wonder what would happen if I should die. But one day the Holy Spirit spoke to me clearly, "My son, why do you try to carry the load yourself? It is too heavy for you. Both you and the ministry I have entrusted to you belong to Me. The church is My Church. You should live in My rest. I have the answers and I know the plans I have designed for My Church and how to fulfill them. You should live totally by My grace and rest in Me."

That revelation into my heart totally revolutionized my life. I felt the heaviness of concern lift from my shoulders. I envisioned myself in His yoke. I truly understood the meaning of the Word, "Take my yoke upon you..." I realized again I was in the yoke with Jesus Christ and He was leading me in every situation. I was only following as He led through the unknown paths. I began to cry, "Father, I never realized You were such a wonderful Father that You would actually carry all the burdens of this work upon Yourself. From today, I am turning over my cares and concerns to You and I will just worship You, love You and commune with You. When the burdens come, I will take time to pray until I can truly release them to You and I will allow You to carry them and work them out."

Yes, sometimes it does take time to release our burdens because we are living in a very independent world. But it can be done.

Friends, Jesus wants to carry your burdens today no matter what they may be. Let the Holy Spirit remind you of the Word, "Take my yoke upon you" and labor to enter into the rest He provided just for His children.